Iron Shirt
Chi Kung

Iron Shirt Chi Kung

Mantak Chia

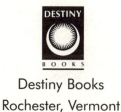

Destiny Books
Rochester, Vermont

Destiny Books
One Park Street
Rochester, Vermont 05767
www.DestinyBooks.com

Destiny Books is a division of Inner Traditions International

Originally published in Thailand in 1986 by Universal Tao Publications under the title *Iron Shirt Chi Kung 1*

Library of Congress Cataloging-in-Publication Data

Chia, Mantak, 1944–
    Iron shirt chi kung / Mantak Chia.
        p. cm.
    "Originally published in Thailand in 1986 by Universal Tao Publications under the title Iron shirt chi kung 1."
    ISBN-13: 978-1-59477-104-0
    ISBN-10: 1-59477-104-9
    1. Kung fu. 2. Health—Religious aspects—Taoism. I. Title.
    GV1114.7.C484 2006
    796.815'9—dc22

                                                                2006010413

Printed and bound in the United States by Versa Press, inc.

20 19 18 17 16 15 14 13 12

Text design and layout by Priscilla Baker
This book was typeset in Janson, with Present, Sho, and Futura used as display typefaces

Contents

Acknowledgments

I thank foremost those Taoist Masters who were kind enough to share their knowledge with me, never imagining it would eventually be taught to Westerners. I acknowledge special thanks to Roberta Prada and Roderick Kettlewell for encouraging the production of this book, for their input on the original manuscript, and for their editing regarding technical procedures.

I thank the many contributors essential to this book's final form: Susan Davidson, editor at Inner Traditions/Destiny Books, for her many contributions to clarifying the text; the artist, Juan Li, for many hours spent drawing, making illustrations of the body's internal functions; Terry Goss for his chapter on the relationships between breath and structural alignment, which helps tremendously in understanding the practice of Iron Shirt; Larry Short for sharing some of the Tibetan Nui Kung Exercises; Michael Brosnahan for helping to clarify the technical points of structure; Dr. Michael Posner for sharing his view of chiropractic and Iron Shirt; and Gunther Weil, Ph.D., Rylin Malone, and many of my students for their feedback.

For their assistance in producing the original edition of this book, I thank Jo Ann Cutreria, our secretary, for making so many contacts and working endlessly; Daniel Bobek for long hours at the computer; John-Robert Zielinski for setting up the new computer system and for his interview of Michael Winn; Valerie Meszaros for editing the book, organizing, typing, and revising it on the computer, and proofreading; Helen Stites for proofreading; Adam Sacks, our computer consultant, who assisted in solving computer problems as they arose during the final stages of production; Michael Winn for general editing, and Cathy Umphress for design and paste ups. Special thanks are extended to David Miller for overseeing design and production of the original edition and to Felix Morrow for his valuable advice and help in editing and producing this book and for agreeing to be the original publisher of Universal Tao Publications.

Without my son, Max, the book would have been academic; for his gifts, my gratitude and love.

Putting Iron Shirt Chi Kung into Practice

The practices described in this book have been used successfully for thousands of years by Taoists trained by personal instruction. Readers should not undertake these practices without receiving personal instruction from a certified instructor of the Universal Tao, because some of these practices, if done improperly, may cause injury or result in health problems. This book is intended to supplement individual training by a Universal Tao instructor and to serve as a reference guide for Universal Tao practices. Anyone who undertakes these practices on the basis of this book alone does so entirely at his or her own risk. Universal Tao instructors can be located at our websites: www.universal-tao.com or www.taoinstructors.org.

The practices of Iron Shirt Chi Kung are very powerful and therefore very effective. To ensure that you carry them out properly, prepare yourself first by learning the Microcosmic Orbit Meditation, the Inner Smile, and the Six Healing Sounds. These will enable you to identify and eliminate energy blockages that may occur in your Iron Shirt practice during the learning stages. Also, practice the preliminary exercises until you are proficient at them and comfortable with them. This will give you the conditioning you need to proceed comfortably to the Iron Shirt Chi Kung postures.

The meditations, practices, and techniques described herein are *not* intended to be used as an alternative or substitute for professional medical treatment and care. If a reader is suffering from a mental or emotional disorder, he or she should consult with an appropriate professional health care practitioner or therapist. Such problems should be corrected before one starts training.

This book does not attempt to give any medical diagnosis, treatment, prescription, or remedial recommendation in relation to any human disease, ailment, suffering, or physical condition whatsoever.

Chinese medicine and Chi Kung emphasize balancing and strengthening the body so that it can heal itself. The meditations, internal exercises, and martial arts of the Universal Tao are basic approaches to this end. Follow the instructions for each exercise carefully. Also pay special attention to the warnings and suggestions. People who have high blood pressure, heart disease, or a generally weak condition should proceed cautiously, having received prior consent from a qualified medical practitioner. People with venereal disease should not attempt any practices involving sexual energy until they are free of the condition.

The Universal Tao and its staff and instructors cannot be responsible for the consequences of any practice or misuse of the information in this book. If the reader undertakes any exercise without strictly following the instructions, notes, and warnings, the responsibility must lie solely with the reader.

Iron Shirt Chi Kung and the Universal Tao

In addition to the more popularly known martial arts disciplines of Kung Fu and Tai Chi, the Universal Tao System includes practices for vibrant health, the development of a state of mindfulness, and the management of vital energy—one's chi. The martial arts aspect of this training, the practice of Iron Shirt Chi Kung, develops a highly refined spiritual awareness.

The goal of the Universal Tao System is to keep our bodies in good condition on the physical plane in order to build and store chi energy for use at the higher level of the spiritual plane. The aim of the human spirit in the spiritual plane is to develop the immortal fetus. This is accomplished in two stages. The first stage is concerned with overcoming reincarnation; the second and final stage concerns educating the immortal fetus toward becoming a full-grown immortal spirit.

Iron Shirt is one of the most important exercises to master on the physical plane. Through Iron Shirt practice the student learns rootedness to Mother Earth energy, a phenomenon intrinsic to the spiritual plane (fig. 1.1). We can compare the rootedness of the physical body to a control tower, vital to the travel of a space shuttle (fig. 1.2). To boost the shuttle—the spirit—into space, the control tower on Earth requires a booster rocket—in this case the soul, or energy body—

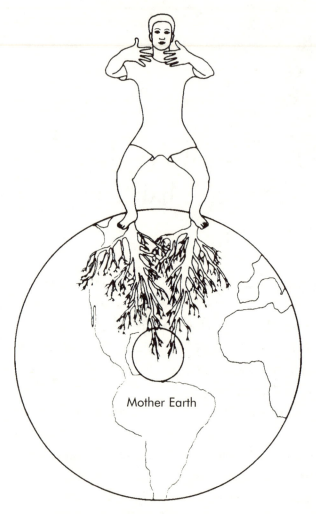

Fig. 1.1. Iron Shirt practice teaches rootedness to Mother Earth.

which is guided by an inner compass and computer—the pineal gland. The control tower, in the form of the physical body developed during the practice of Iron Shirt, becomes a storage place for fuel—that fuel being our chi (life-force energy) and our creative, or sexual, energy.

In our Iron Shirt body our fuel awaits transformation into another kind of energy: spiritual energy. Yet we must maintain our foundation, our rootedness to the Earth, so that as we learn to travel to the

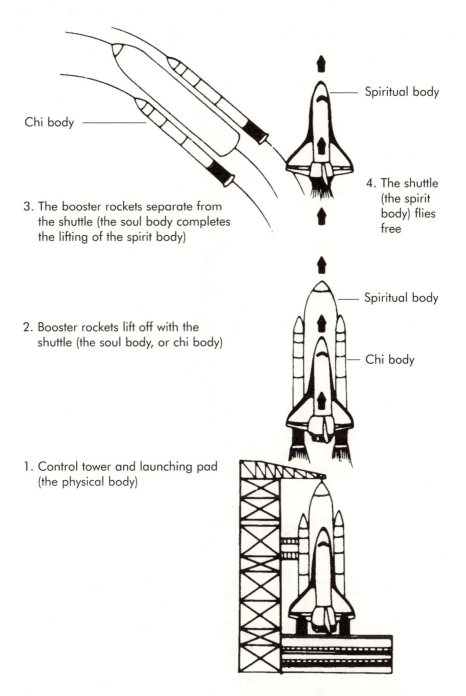

Chi body

Spiritual body

3. The booster rockets separate from the shuttle (the soul body completes the lifting of the spirit body)

4. The shuttle (the spirit body) flies free

Spiritual body

Chi body

2. Booster rockets lift off with the shuttle (the soul body, or chi body)

1. Control tower and launching pad (the physical body)

Fig. 1.2. Launching the spiritual body through rooting to the Earth

immortal realms we are able to return to Earth and refuel our bodies (fig. 1.3). From there we can resume our travel to our destination until, eventually, we are able to discard the earthly base entirely.

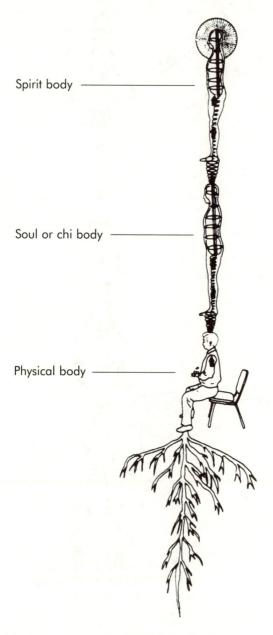

Spirit body

Soul or chi body

Physical body

Fig. 1.3. Rootedness

IRON SHIRT CHI KUNG, AN ANCIENT KUNG FU PRACTICE

Kung Fu was practiced in China long before the advent of firearms. During the Bolin Period, approximately 1000 BC, training in the various spiritual/martial arts was quite intense. It is said that at the time one-tenth of the population of China was involved in some sort of Kung Fu training.

Training began in very early youth. The student first worked to develop internal power, or inner strength through organ exercises, an endeavor that could take as long as ten years. In ancient times internal power was cultivated until it could be felt flowing out of the hands. With weights tied to the legs, the practitioner ran and jumped in prescribed ways for over three hours a day until, eventually, he could jump easily to great heights while at the same time further developing his internal power. Only after these exercises were mastered were actual fighting techniques taught.

Iron Shirt Chi Kung, a method of Kung Fu, was taught as a protective training, one that provided internal power through the practice of external techniques. The Iron Shirt practitioner was protected against the effects of blows to his vital organs and glands, the primary places where life-force energy, or chi, is produced. Being on the receiving end of internal power in martial arts can be compared to being struck by a steel rod as opposed to one that is made of soft plastic. The Chi Kung practitioner of old practiced one punch for years until he could feel the power go out of the lower part of his hand while the rest of his body seemed as though made of steel.

There were many other benefits as well—internal power improved general health and is thought to have maintained youthfulness. The development of internal power also helped to perfect mental faculties, enabling the practitioner to have knowledge of many things. One reads that during the Bolin Period there were eight "immortals" who spent most of their lives in the practice of internal power and developed extraordinary abilities as a result. They could predict the future and see into the past. They are said to have been capable of space travel and of clairvoyance and clairaudience. It is also said that during that period many people had at least some such powers, a result of widespread Kung Fu practice.

With the invention of gunpowder and the subsequent development of firearms, men no longer felt the need to spend a decade or more of their lives learning skills that suddenly seemed impractical and unnecessary. With firearms as weapons a man could now defend himself, or at the least cause great damage, while standing at a great distance from his enemy.

Contact fighting became a thing of the past, and much knowledge that was useful to humanity was lost with it. Today, however, as people begin to recognize the depersonalizing and unhealthy effects of technology, there has been a revival of interest in the simpler ways of life. Thus Kung Fu, a means of perfecting the inner self, is once again in the limelight.

CREATING CHI PRESSURE WITH IRON SHIRT BREATHING

The word *kung* means discipline. The word *chi* refers to the energy derived from breathing the oxygen (20 percent) and the inert nitrogen (78 percent) of the air. *Chi* also refers to the subtle vital energy of Earth, nature, and the universe.

Chi Kung is the practice of breathing to increase chi pressure in the body. Chi breathing is coordinated with breathing the air in and out of the physical body; with practice the practitioner becomes sensitive to the chi and learns to work with it. Chi Kung can be thought of as internal aerobics. Chi, in the form of an aerobic energy involving air, steam, and pressure, presses out and circulates to protect the internal body. We can compare the internal pressure created by Chi Kung to the force of air in a tire that is sufficient to keep the tire inflated and to maintain a cushion between the car and the road (fig. 1.4).

Breathing is the most important aspect of bodily life. We can go

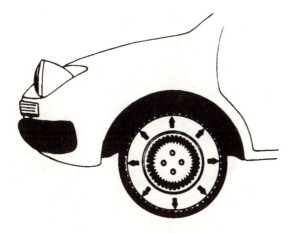

Fig. 1.4. The internal pressure created by chi can be compared
to the cushioning provided by an inflated tire.

without food for months and we can go without water for days, but
we can go without air for only a few minutes before we expire. In Iron
Shirt Chi Kung we use our breath to maximum advantage. Through
breathing exercises we increase our vital energy, strengthen our
organs, and promote self-healing by increasing the chi pressure (the
pounds per square inch, using our metaphor of an inflated tire) in the
organs and cavity of the body. The circulatory system, the lymphatic
system, the nervous system, and the endocrine glands become activated and blood, spinal fluid, and hormones flow more easily.

Taoists believe that as fetuses growing in the womb we use Iron
Shirt Packing Breathing. Before birth the infant does not use the
lungs and nose to breathe. Instead, chi enters the navel through the
umbilical cord, then travels down to the perineum, up the sacrum
and through the spinal cord to the head and forehead, and then
travels down the front of the body from the tongue* to the throat,
heart, abdomen, and navel centers, where the chi pressure can be
used (fig. 1.5). You will recognize the path described here as the path

---

* Taoists believe the fetus holds the tongue on the palate, which is an important link-
ing point in connecting energy between the back and the front of the body.

Fig. 1.5. In an unborn infant the chi (life force) enters the
navel through the umbilical cord.

of the Microcosmic Orbit. Moving the chi through the Microcosmic Orbit is a fundamental practice in the Universal Tao system that is described more fully in chapter 2.

At birth we begin to use lung breathing, generating our own energy rather than utilizing this internal source of energy. In the beginning of our life on Earth our lungs are not strong; the abdomen, being closer to our original source of energy—the navel—has more chi pressure than the lungs. Thus the abdomen assists the lungs with breathing by pulling down on the diaphragm on the inhalation, so that the lower portion of the lungs can fill with air. In this way the lungs use less energy but take in more life force (oxygen).

As children we continue to use abdominal chi-pressure energy. But we can see the effects of reduced chi pressure that come along with age. In older people the prenatal life force (chi) is drained out of the navel and kidney areas. Gradually chi pressure is lost, creating an energy imbalance: when the pressure is low the fluid flow in the entire system slows down. As a result, at the times when our energy becomes too hot it moves up and creates congestion in the chest and head. Cold energy moves down through the sexual organs and leaks out; we gradually lose chi pressure in that manner too.

As we age we also begin to lose the habit of abdominal breathing. The lungs are left to do all the breathing through the chest, which is an inefficient way to breathe. Chest breathing requires using greater energy to expand the rib cage and is only sufficient for filling the upper one-third of the lungs. This method of breathing actually expends more energy than it creates. Scientists have affirmed that, with chest breathing, we use only one-third of our lung capacity for breathing; then, yielding to gravitational pressure, our organs collapse. With abdominal breathing we can expand the amount of pressure exerted on the internal organs and strengthen the organs by voluntarily compressing and releasing them.

WHY PUT ON YOUR IRON SHIRT?

Many of the physical changes associated with Kung Fu come through managing the internal organs and endocrine glands. In Kung Fu practice a person's life force is said to depend primarily upon the endocrine glands and the hormones they produce.

Consider what happens when a person is deprived of a fully functional endocrine system. For example, a male is radically altered when his testes are eliminated, and more so when this occurs before puberty. The characteristics that result are weak musculature and fat-distribution patterns more common to females. Depending upon the time in life in which a male loses his testes he might also lack secondary male characteristics, such as a deep voice, facial hair, and typical sexual drive. It is well documented that male and female castrates have shortened life spans.

With Iron Shirt Chi Kung the practitioner is able to increase the flow of hormones produced by the endocrine glands, thus building up the immune system and developing a general sense of well-being. The sexual energy (that is, creative energy) produced by Iron Shirt Chi Kung is another source of chi energy that may later be transformed into spiritual energy.

Integral to Iron Shirt are exercises that cleanse and strengthen the organs. Strong, detoxified organs are important to living a full and healthy life. Iron Shirt practice will strengthen the organs; help to clean out toxins, waste materials, and sediment in the organs; and convert the fat stored in layers of connective tissue (fascia) into chi energy. The chi is then stored in these connective tissue layers, where it works like a cushion to protect the organs. As previously mentioned, this process can be compared to a tire which, when inflated with air, can sustain tremendous weight. Chi that has been stored in such a way not only protects the body but becomes available for transformation to a higher-quality energy that can nourish the soul and spirit.

In the practice of Iron Shirt we focus on the connective tissue (the fascia), organs, tendons, bones, and bone marrow more than we emphasize developing the musculature.

The body may be seen as consisting of three layers: the innermost layer, which is made up of the internal organs that produce chi; a layer consisting of fascia, bones, and tendons; and the muscles, which constitute the outer bulk of the body. After being developed in the internal organs, chi is distributed throughout the fascia. It is with the fascia that Iron Shirt I is primarily concerned.*

---

* This book is concerned with the first level of Iron Shirt Chi Kung practice, in which the fascia is energized through internal exercises. Iron Shirt Chi Kung II is a practice known since ancient times as Changing the Tendons. This practice utilizes the mind and heart to direct, stretch, and grow the tendons. Iron Shirt Chi Kung III works on bone structure and increases the bone marrow. This process, known by the ancient Taoists as Cleansing the Marrow, is used to clear out fat stored in the hollow bone and absorb the creative power (sexual energy) into the bone to rebuild the bone marrow. This is a most beneficial practice, since bones are the major blood builders, including the builders of white blood cells, necessary to the body's defense mechanisms.

Iron Shirt Energizes the Fasciae

Every cell, every muscle, and every organ in the body is covered by a membranous sheath, or fascia (fig. 1.6). Connecting every tissue of the body, the fascia links the various parts of the inner body into an integrated whole. The fascia that covers the heart, lungs, stomach, liver, kidneys, and all the other organs of the body has protective, regenerative, and nourishing properties. The fascia acts as an energizing chamber for the organ.

In the therapeutic bodywork techniques of Hellerwork and Rolfing, the fascia is worked from the outside in. Rolfing involves freeing layers of fascia that have become stuck together through trauma, infection,

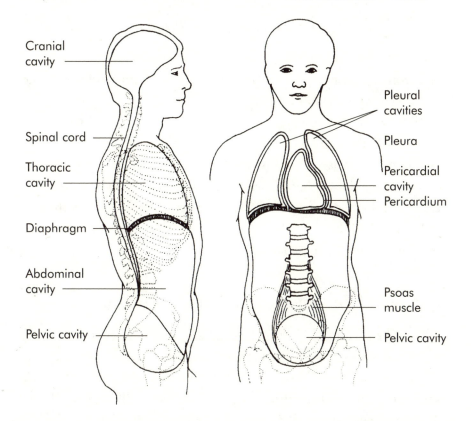

Fig. 1.6. Each organ in the body has a fascial layer covering it.

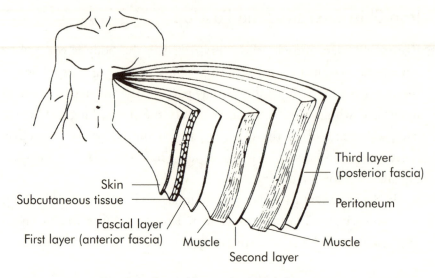

Fig. 1.7. Fascial layers in the abdomen

or chronic muscular tensions. In contrast, Iron Shirt works from the inner layer of fascia outward (fig. 1.7).

The fascia is extremely important in the practice of Iron Shirt because, as the most pervasive tissue in the body, it is believed to be the means whereby chi is distributed along acupuncture routes. Research has shown that the least resistance to the flow of bioelectric energy in the body occurs between the fascial sheaths. When the fascial routes have been charted, they have been found to correspond to the classic acupuncture channels.

Iron Shirt Strengthens and Protects the Organs

When filled with chi pressure, the fascial layers covering the organs will act as energizers for the organs. Extra chi pressure will escape to the abdominal fascial layer and fill the abdominal cavity. When the abdominal cavity fills with chi pressure, that chi will start to fill the deep fascia and, finally, fill in the outer layer of fascia, acting as a triple layer or cushion that protects all of the organs, muscles, and glands.

To better understand how the fascia, the organs, and chi relate to one another, picture an egg residing inside an air-filled balloon, which itself resides inside another air-filled balloon, both of which reside inside one more air-filled balloon (fig. 1.8). An egg is normally quite vulnerable, but inside an air-filled balloon it is cushioned against blows. The egg has even greater protection inside a triple layer of balloons: you can throw and kick these balloons and the egg will remain unharmed.

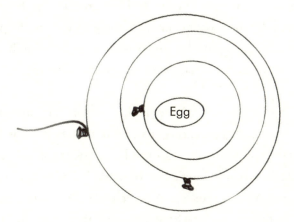

Fig. 1.8. Air-filled balloons protect an egg as the
chi-filled fascia protects the organs.

Chi and the fascia act in the same way to protect the fragile organs. Fascia is elastic and protective, like balloons. The chi, expanding as the air expands within the balloons, creates pressure to fill the fascia, which surround the organs like the balloons surround the egg. People who are so unlucky as to be struck in their vital organs can become seriously injured. When the vital organs are injured, life is endangered. But you greatly reduce the risk of unexpected injury with the practice of building layers of protection into the organs. You might even save your own life. When chi pressure is reduced by sickness or a weakened constitution, the organs collapse in upon themselves, becoming compressed and energy deficient.

From the fascia, Iron Shirt extends to involve the bones and tendons and, finally, the muscles.

Iron Shirt Burns Fat
and Strengthens Bones

Food (nutrition) that is taken into the body but is not required by the body is turned into fat and stored in the outer layers of fascia. This fat will greatly reduce the conduction of chi throughout the body. The Iron Shirt Packing Process helps to condense and squeeze the fat, transforming it into energy to be stored in the fascial covers of the organs for use whenever it is needed. When chi pressure occupies the fascial layers, fat cannot be stored there. The body thus becomes trained to convert fat into chi energy for storage in the fascial layers.

When the fascia is filled with chi, the tendons are strengthened and the bones hold together as one structural unit. When the fascia is weak the muscles are weakened and the bone structure will not hold together. Similarly, when the muscles are weak, both the fascia and the tendons are weak. When muscles are not used they diminish in size and strength, as does the fascia that contains them and the tendons upon which they pull when activated.

The human body is an amazing organism. New cells are being generated all the time to replenish old and dying tissues. There is a constant turnover of most of the cells of the body, and replacements are governed by ongoing needs. It has been demonstrated that during prolonged periods of weightlessness in outer space, the constitution of bones is not as dense as it is on the surface of the Earth, where the greater stresses of gravity signal the body to develop heavier bone growth. When we are young our bones are filled with marrow (fig. 1.9). Through adulthood the bones gradually hollow out, filling with fat and producing fewer blood cells, until they become brittle and susceptible to fracture. Iron Shirt Chi Kung is designed to gradually reabsorb the chi life force back into the bones, which can then be transformed into bone marrow to strengthen the bone structure.

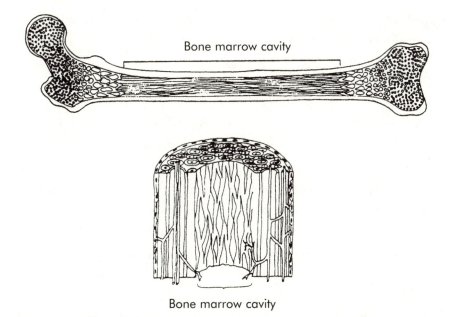

Bone marrow cavity

Bone marrow cavity

Fig. 1.9. New blood cells are created in the shaft of the bones;
with age the shaft hollows out. Iron Shirt practices absorb chi
back into the bones, strengthening the skeletal structure.

Iron Shirt Increases Circulation while Reducing the Heart's Work

As mentioned earlier, we must learn to use the abdomen to aid in breathing and to help increase circulation. The abdominal area accounts for two-thirds of the blood supply that flows through the liver, kidneys, stomach, and spleen. With proper training the abdomen can act as the most efficient heart you could ever have.

With the Packing Process breathing practice taught in Iron Shirt Chi Kung, you limit the space inside the abdominal cavity and increase the pounds of pressure per square inch, squeezing all the organs in the abdominal area into a very small space. This process expels the toxins and sediment that have accumulated in these organs. With each inhalation the diaphragm pulls down farther and farther into the abdominal cavity while the abdomen remains flat. The descent of the diaphragm creates a vacuum in the lower part of the lungs, filling the lower lobes, and eventually the entire lung area, with fresh oxygen. The longer, deeper breaths deliver a sufficient quantity of oxygen to cleanse the body of waste materials, sediment, and toxins.

The body's internal system relies entirely upon chi pressure to move the fluids. Increased chi pressure in the abdominal cavity helps to move chi, blood, and lymphatic fluids. When fresh blood is released from the heart, oxygen and nutrients travel to and are more efficiently taken in by the organs. With Iron Shirt practice you will gradually increase the fluid flow within the circulatory and lymphatic systems and, in return, you will greatly reduce the work of the heart. As you gradually increase your vital capacity by learning how to pack oxygen into the organs—thereby creating the cushion, or chi pressure, to protect and strengthen the organs—the heart will work with progressively less effort and circulation will increase. The vital energy thus conserved can be used to enrich your spiritual and creative lives.

Our goal, then, is to increase the organ and abdominal pressure so that chi presses outward on the fascial layers from inside. To do this you will learn Packing Process Breathing to increase the pressure of chi in the organs and abdomen. When this pressure is released the fascia expands, as do the organs.

Chi-circulation meditation affords a means of generating and directing far more chi than would ordinarily be possible without causing pressure on the heart. Different from running and other aerobic exercises, meditation increases circulation and the production of lymphocytes without affecting blood pressure. The chi-circulation practice of the Microcosmic Orbit, the foundation for all practices in the Universal Tao system, enables you to identify and eliminate energy blockages in the body. It is essential that you prepare yourself for learning Iron Shirt Chi Kung by first becoming proficient at the Microcosmic Orbit chi-circulation meditation. The Microcosmic Orbit practice will be reviewed in chapter 2. See also my books *Awakening Healing Energy through the Tao* and *Awaken Healing Light of the Tao* for in-depth instruction. Please remember that a book is not a substitute for the depth of instruction and the practice refinements that come through working directly with a teacher.

The energy utilized in Iron Shirt travels along the same route as the Microcosmic Orbit but is found to be expressed differently in each of the channels. As the chi flows more freely throughout the entire body, the experience takes on new dimensions.

It is currently believed by many here in the West that daily physical exercise helps to stave off aging. However, it is questionable whether athletes live longer or are appreciably healthier for their efforts. In fact, as the effects of aging impede their physical abilities, many athletes become subject to depression because they are no longer able to compete successfully.

Taoists believe that chi can be transformed into any substance or tissue in the body. The energy we channel in the body has a generative effect. Taoist practices such as Microcosmic Orbit Chi-Circulation, Iron Shirt breathing and packing, Stem Cell Chi Kung, Sexual Energy Cultivation, and Bone Marrow Nei Kung provide the basis for repairing, regenerating, improving, and preserving cells of the organs, brain, and all body parts. This results in greater vitality and functionality and extended longevity.

Taoists in the past did not have the benefit of information now emerging from the fields of genetics, stem cell research, cryogenics, and the subatomic realm of quantum mechanics that corroborates the potentials inherent within the human body and the universal energy field. Through personal exploration, proceeding in the "unnameable" way of the Tao, they developed physical methods that enabled them to attain phenomenal results. They learned to cultivate and refine the mysterious vital energy of life that came to be referred to as *chi*, and they experienced the amazing and beneficial effects of that cultivation. All that they achieved came about by attuning themselves to the chi.

Iron Shirt Prevents Energy Leakages and Prolongs Life

Long life and happiness have been pursued by people for centuries, and the search goes on. Man's life span has been prolonged by science and technology; however, more often than not the added years can be of substandard quality.

Modern society emphasizes material aspects of life, whereas the ancient Taoists sought to balance the material with the spiritual. The old Taoist sages say that in ancient times men lived from between five hundred to one thousand years. The Taoist and yogic approaches describe an "inner world" that human beings can develop and cultivate, which is then reflected in the outer world.

An important function of Iron Shirt is to learn how to create space in the body to store chi energy and to learn how to prevent energy leakage. For most people energy is dispersed and scattered throughout the body, and it escapes through various openings in the body. Iron Shirt teaches the practitioner how to seal these body openings and how to direct this conserved energy to the navel region, there to be packed and condensed into an energy ball that can be directed to any part of the body (fig. 1.10).

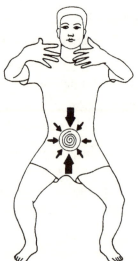

Fig. 1.10. Concentrating energy into an energy ball at the navel

Practices such as Iron Shirt Chi Kung can prolong life in such a way that it is vital and satisfying to the end. The Taoist system is very precise in the matter of building chi, guiding that chi, and developing skills to make the best use of the chi. To attempt to hasten the process by skipping steps is to end with nothing or to create complications such as irregular heartbeat; chest congestion; headache; and pain in the heart, chest, or back that result from not knowing how to guide the energy.

SUMMARY OF THE BENEFITS OF IRON SHIRT CHI KUNG TRAINING

In summary, Iron Shirt Chi Kung I training is divided into three aspects: the physical, the emotional, and the spiritual. On the physical level we learn how to:

- Strengthen and alter a weak structure into a strong one so that chi can flow easily throughout the body and provide room for organs to grow within the body's structure
- Develop a chi belt, the major point of connection between upper and lower energy channels, without which proper structural alignment and chi energy will be lost
- Detoxify and exercise the organs and glands in order to charge and pack the chi in them, to serve as cushioning to surround and protect the organs and glands and to fill the cavity of the body with chi pressure
- Increase chi storage between the fascial sheets; open the fasciae to serve as chi storage areas of the body, replacing fat previously stored there; and understand the function of the fascial layers as cushions around the body that protect the vital organs
- Condense life-force energy into a ball, enabling practitioners to control their chi so that the chi will not scatter around the body and leak out of the system

- Root down and become one with the Earth, passing the body's force down to Earth without obstruction, and then to pump the Earth force up into the structure and counteract outside forces with the assistance of Earth's energy
- Generate an easily flowing chi through the meridians of the body and transform chi to a higher "octane" to serve as the nourishment for the soul and spirit body

On the emotional level, or soul level, one learns how to condense the chi into a controllable mass of energy, transforming and moving the chi by changing negative energy into positive energy. Condensed chi has more power to be used as a person desires. When you are well trained in condensing the chi energy into a ball by physically moving the abdomen up and down or left and right, you will begin being able to use your mind to move that chi ball and direct it through channels in your body, always returning it to the navel. In these higher levels of practice the condensed chi becomes a light ball, like a glowing pearl, which develops into the energy body, serving as a rocket to boost the spirit, or space body, into orbit.

On the spiritual level Iron Shirt Chi Kung condenses, strengthens, and creates more chi, thereby laying the groundwork for a spiritual foundation or rootedness. Previously likened to a control tower, this foundation will direct the spirit in its journey through space, where preparations are made for life after death.

The Iron Shirt exercises introduced in this book are primarily concerned with the fascial and bone structures of the body as well as with some tendons. These eight exercises, condensed from forty-nine postures, are very precise in developing the most vital energy routes in the body. Many exercises will serve this purpose; however, by doing the eight exercises and the structural alignment practices described in this book you will derive as much benefit as you would from a wider selection of positions and movements.

The eight exercises are:

1. Embracing the Tree
2. Holding the Golden Urn, Yang Position
3. Holding the Golden Urn, Yin Position
4. The Golden Turtle Immersing in Water
5. The Water Buffalo Emerging from Water
6. The Golden Phoenix Washes Its Feathers
7. Iron Bridge
8. Iron Bar

In the tradition of Taoist esoteric yoga it is said that chi moves the blood (and so the heart works less); blood moves muscles; muscles move tendons; and tendons move the bones to which they are attached. These exercises develop chi flow and strengthen fascia, tendons, bones, and muscles.

Iron Shirt strengthens muscles, tendons, and bones by subjecting them directly and gradually to increasing stress. It is a well-rounded approach that, as an additional benefit, offers a means of releasing long-held areas of tension. This often reflects in a general sense of well being, self-assurance, and ease, along with better posture.

Many of my students report that Iron Shirt has enabled them to achieve a deep sense of groundedness. Others suddenly discover that their hands and feet are no longer chronically cold. There is another advantage to Iron Shirt. The pneumatic effect joins what would otherwise be felt as separate aspects of the body into one continuous unit, creating a unified and integrated alignment of the skeletal structure such that enormous physical force can be easily transferred through the structure to and from the ground with a minimum of muscular exertion. This produces a tremendous increase in mechanical strength that increases exponentially as this work progresses.

Iron Shirt Chi Kung is the foundation for Tai Chi, which uses structural alignment as a basis for exercise. Many people have the wrong idea about Tai Chi. When chi energy is generated during Tai Chi movements the practitioner wants to move that energy. However, the moving form of Tai Chi occupies the mind with many things other than moving energy. The more that practitioners put their bodies in motion, the busier their minds become, making them less aware of the subtle energy that can be felt within. Conversely, the more simple a practitioner keeps the activities of the mind, the better the practitioner can feel his or her inner workings.

The Universal Tao System offers many types of training, several of which can be practiced individually. However, all of the Universal Tao teachings are interrelated, and practicing them together will bring the best results. A person who attempts to practice Tai Chi Chuan before having first cultivated internal energy through Iron Shirt might be compared with a student entering high school without having learned the alphabet.

Iron Shirt uses the mind to guide the chi flow while the body stays in a more or less static position. If you train in the methods of Iron Shirt first you learn well how to move chi. Then when you practice Tai Chi it becomes easier to move chi while keeping the mind engaged with the moving forms. In the Universal Tao system we require students to first learn the Microcosmic Orbit and then Iron Shirt Chi Kung before they learn Tai Chi. The structural rooting and energy discharge and control that is learned in Iron Shirt can be transferred to the Tai Chi form. It should also be noted that to practice Tai Chi Chuan properly, it is necessary that your meditation practice take you at least to the levels in the Universal Tao system of Fusion of the Five Elements or to Lesser Enlightenment Kan and Li.

Since the basic approaches of the Microcosmic Orbit, Iron Shirt Chi Kung, Seminal or Ovarian Kung Fu, and Tai Chi Chi Kung deal with some aspect of coaxing energy out of the deepest and innermost reaches of the body, it is wise for the practitioner who is interested in developing fully his physical, emotional, and spiritual potentials to consider studying the Universal Tao system in its entirety.

Preparations for Iron Shirt Chi Kung

Iron Shirt breathing practice combines various types of breathing. The success of the Iron Shirt Chi Kung exercises depends upon mind control and relaxation. You must not use force in any of these practices. For example, when pressing the chin down to the chest and pushing outward at C7, the chest must remain relaxed if you are not to develop chest pain and congestion and if you are to avoid difficulty in breathing. Practice the Inner Smile relaxation technique and run your Microcosmic Orbit. (These practices are described briefly in this chapter and more fully in the book *Awaken Healing Energy through the Tao*.)

During various phases of Iron Shirt Chi Kung practice, especially in the beginning stages of training, there is a natural tendency to tense (tighten) muscle tissue in larger areas of the body, beyond the isolated area you may be exercising with focused contractions and pressure. The practitioner must therefore be ever mindful of not building unwanted tension in those extraneous areas, and instead learn to relax and release. Chronic tension blocks chi flow and results in unhealthy conditions that should be resolved in order to ensure physical and emotional equanimity.

Inducing positively focused tension in some phases of Iron Shirt Chi Kung training and then consciously releasing that tension may in fact help to avoid dire future consequences. Along with the purposely induced tension, chronically acquired tension can also be released in the process, serving to avoid the development of cancer or heart attacks, as extreme examples. Once a practitioner has learned the Inner Smile meditative process, it is a simple matter to activate the relaxation response through the parasympathetic nervous system and to radiate the gentle smiling sensation to release tensed areas.

In regard to the constructive use of tension and pressure in one's practice, thoughts such as "not too much and not too little" and "be soft like a baby, yet sturdy as steel" would be good to keep in mind. Stay within your comfort zone! Just as a child can learn to chew gum, talk, and ride a bicycle all at the same time, the Iron Shirt practitioner can maintain a comfortable balance of tension and pressure with relaxation and healthy chi flow. Be patient and stay balanced. Use the Inner Smile and Microcosmic Orbit circulation as part of the practice whenever they are needed. If you find yourself shaking and jerking about, just simply let that happen. Shaking and jerking are good omens, resulting from the movement of chi opening blockages in meridians that affect muscles in the area. The muscular spasms subside when the chi flow stabilizes. It is a refreshing experience.

At any time during this practice you can relieve congestion that might accumulate at the chest by stroking your chest with your palms from top to bottom from 9 to 18 times. Burp if the need arises. If you find yourself salivating copiously, tighten your neck muscles, press your chin to your chest, and smile downward through all of your organs. Then put your tongue to your palate and, using force, swallow saliva so that you feel as though you have indeed swallowed all the way down to your navel. Concentrate there until you can feel your navel grow warm.

Practice the Iron Shirt Chi Kung breathing exercises as outlined in this chapter twice per day during your first week of practice and 3 times per day in the following week. By the third to fourth week you can increase your daily practice to 6 to 9 times in a day and increase the length of time you spend practicing Packing Breathing.

ABDOMINAL BREATHING AND REVERSE BREATHING (ENERGIZER BREATHING)

We begin the practice of Packing Process Breathing by learning abdominal breathing, which energizes and loosens the fascial layers of the body. Abdominal breathing and reverse breathing are the two basic modes of breath training. When practiced together they are known as Energizer Breathing; in yoga this union of breath practices is called Breath of Fire or Bellows Breathing.

Abdominal and reverse breathing take place by virtue of the up-and-down movement of the thoracic diaphragm (fig. 2.1). In abdominal breathing the diaphragm lowers, forcing the vital organs, especially the kidneys and adrenal glands, to compress downward and allowing the lower lobes of the lungs to fill with air, forcing the abdomen outward. The chest and the sternum sink, pressing on and activating the thymus gland, an important site of hormone production in support of the body's immune-system functioning. Upon exhalation the abdomen returns to its flatter shape and the other vital organs return to their original sizes and shapes.

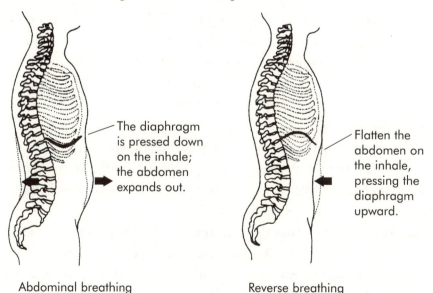

The diaphragm is pressed down on the inhale; the abdomen expands out.

Flatten the abdomen on the inhale, pressing the diaphragm upward.

Abdominal breathing   Reverse breathing

Fig. 2.1. Movement of the diaphragm during breathing

Most people who have not had Taoist, yogic, or other similar deep-breathing training find it awkward and disorienting at first to coordinate the movements of the thoracic diaphragm and the abdomen in abdominal breathing. The physical movements of the chest and sternum, combined with intentionally pressing the thoracic diaphragm more forcefully downward while simultaneously expanding the abdominal musculature outward as you inhale more air into the fully expanding lower lobes of the lungs, actually require a fair amount of muscle and tendon coordination and exertion. Of course, these various exertions result in a most beneficial massage for all of the affected organs, glands, and lymph nodes in the chest and abdominal areas. But even for experienced practitioners who enjoy the peace, pleasure, and enhanced vitality of this more profound mode of breathing, it takes a few breath cycles to shift gears from the "normal" upper-lungs form of breathing. This transitional process of adjustment from the lighter, more superficial, quicker rhythm of "normal" breathing to the slow, smooth, steady, conscious deep-abdominal breathing is what we refer to as "harmonizing the breath."

Harmonizing the breath with abdominal breathing is about much more than simply improving the efficiency and effectiveness of absorbing oxygen and nitrogen from the air. It lessens the strain on the heart and improves blood circulation throughout the body, in effect creating a second heart. It also opens the lower, mostly unused area of the lungs—the largest part of the lungs, in fact—improving their effectiveness.

Furthermore, Taoist "harmonizing the breath" coordinates breathing the subtle chi (vital energy) of Earth, nature, and the universe into the tan tien center, the central chi-storage area behind the navel. Apart from improving the process of breathing air into the lungs, perhaps the more significant aspect of harmonizing the breath is that it trains our "second brain" in the abdomen, the enteric nervous system, to take command as the control center for subtle chi breathing and for storing chi in the abdomen, where it can then be used by the whole body. This feat is to be accomplished by the gentle force of the practitioner's intention and focused attention via inner feeling and awareness. By gathering chi and strengthening the reserves of chi in the abdominal center, the practitioner gains access to the life force that enables mastery of health and the mechanism of personal evolution.

When the breath is harmonized, chi is sent down to the navel; then reverse breathing is initiated. Reverse breathing is the starting point for the Packing Breath. Rather than expanding on the inhale, in reverse breathing the abdomen flattens on the inhale. Flattening the abdomen pushes the organs and the diaphragm upward.

With Packing Process Breathing you actively maintain a *lowered* diaphragm. The flat abdomen and lowered diaphragm compress the organs and minimize the space inside the abdominal cavity. Squeezing the organs in this way expels toxins and sediments that have built up in the organs.

We begin our practice of Packing Process Breathing with abdominal breathing, which energizes the navel area and warms up the body for the more difficult practices of reverse breathing and Packing Process Breathing.

Abdominal Breathing Practice

To practice abdominal breathing, keep the chest very relaxed. This may prove difficult at first but it is very important, so keep working at it.

1. Begin by breathing in, drawing air into the lungs and expanding the abdomen. Focus especially on the area $1^{1}/_{2}$ inches below the navel, the main chi-storage site in the body.
2. Make the chest hollow and press the thoracic diaphragm down (fig. 2.2). Pressure is felt inside the abdomen, which will begin to protrude on all sides in a rounded shape. Do not expand the front of the abdomen only—make sure that the sides and back of the abdomen expand as well. With the diaphragm lowered and the abdomen expanded, the upper abdominal space that normally contains the abdominal organs is minimized.

Fig. 2.2. With abdominal breathing you make the chest hollow and press
the diaphragm down, compressing the kidneys and the adrenals.

3. Hold your breath for a moment and then exhale. As you exhale,
   release the diaphragm so that it recedes upward into its relaxed
   dome shape within the lower chest. Relax the expanded abdominal
   musculature, allowing the abdomen to flatten toward the spine.
   Feel the perineum (the region between the genital organs and the
   rectum) flood with the pressure. Pull the sexual organs upward as
   you sink through the chest and sternum, pressing and activating
   the thymus gland (fig. 2.3). Do not use force. It is enough to feel
   a slight pull and flattening of the chest.
4. Inhale and feel the diaphragm drop downward again. Expand the
   abdomen on all sides, like a round ball. Exhale and pull the sexual
   organs upward.
5. With each inhalation and exhalation counting as one set, practice
   each set 9, then 18, and then 36 times. Follow this general rule of

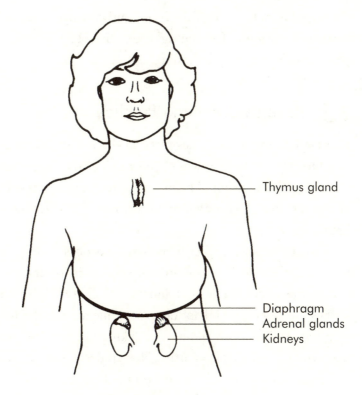

Thymus gland

Diaphragm
Adrenal glands
Kidneys

Fig. 2.3. The thymus gland

thumb: Don't force it. Do what you can comfortably; it gets easier with practice. Increase the repetitions within your personal comfort zone.

Abdominal breathing is used throughout all the Iron Shirt Chi Kung exercises as a warm-up for Packing Process Breathing. It is also used after Packing Process Breathing to regulate the breath.

If you find that your diaphragm is tight and pushed up into the rib cage, massage the diaphragm with both hands, using the fingers to gently work the diaphragm so that it will drop down into a relaxed position.

Tightness in the abdominal area is one of the main causes of breathing problems. Abdominal massage will help to relieve the tightness of the diaphragm. Use your fingers to lightly massage the abdomen at the navel area until you feel the tightness ease. This will greatly improve your capacity for deep breathing.

 ## Reverse Breathing Practice

Reverse breathing also takes place in the lower abdomen—you draw air into the abdomen while contracting the abdominal muscles. Reverse breathing should be practiced in conjunction with abdominal breathing. Begin with abdominal breathing and follow with reverse breathing.

Instead of feeling the diaphragm and organs drop down on the inhale, as they do in abdominal breathing, in reverse breathing you flatten the abdomen on the inhale; the flattening of the abdomen pushes the organs and diaphragm *up* while air fills the lungs. Reverse breathing is the starting point for Packing Process Breathing, in which we maintain the diaphragm in a lowered position. As your practice develops you will be able to control the diaphragm and organs, keeping them lowered while the belly stays flat on the inhalation.

1. To begin reverse breathing, first practice 6 rounds of abdominal breathing. On your last exhalation, flatten the abdomen toward the spine.
2. Maintain the flattened abdomen as you begin reverse breathing. On the inhalation feel the abdomen flatten even more, as if it were pressing toward the spine; focus especially on the area $1\frac{1}{2}$ inches below the navel. Flattening the abdomen will thrust the diaphragm upward; as practice for Packing Process Breathing, resist that by trying to lower the diaphragm and push down on the organs as you continue to tighten the abdomen. Feel the perineum flood with pressure. Pull the sexual organs up.
3. Lowering the diaphragm is the hardest part of this practice. Work at this, utilizing the relaxation technique of smiling to the diaphragm and the abdomen.

4. Exhale, releasing the pressure in the perineum and in the sexual organs. Exhale through the lower abdomen, allowing the pressure to extend the lower abdomen out to all sides. Relax, letting the fascia expand while completely releasing and relaxing the chest. Smile down to your organs. Relax.

5. Counting each inhalation and exhalation as a round, practice reverse breathing for 6 rounds, then 9 rounds, finally working up to 18 rounds. Stay within your comfort zone and increase the repetitions as the body permits. Be persistent, but don't force it. Practice until you are able to control the diaphragm with your mind, commanding it to lower or to lift with your attention and intention, rather than reflexively.

Tight muscles in the chest can be a problem—it is most important to relax. It is relaxation, not muscular power, that keeps the chi packed inside the organs.

THE IMPORTANCE OF THE PELVIC AND UROGENITAL DIAPHRAGMS

Before we build on abdominal and reverse breathing by learning the steps involved in the Iron Shirt Packing Process, let us first take a moment to discuss two other diaphragms that are involved in this breath work.

In addition to the respiratory diaphragm, the human body also contains a pelvic diaphragm and a urogenital diaphragm, both of which are exceedingly important in transmitting energy in Iron Shirt Chi Kung. The pelvic diaphragm is a muscular wall that extends across the lower part of the torso, suspended concavely between the sacrum in back and the pubic symphysis (the joint that connects the pubic bones) in front (fig. 2.4). Several organs penetrate this muscular partition that lies between the pelvic cavity and the perineum: these are the urethra, the vagina, and the rectum, all of which are supported by the pelvic diaphragm. In fact, the pelvic diaphragm is the floor of

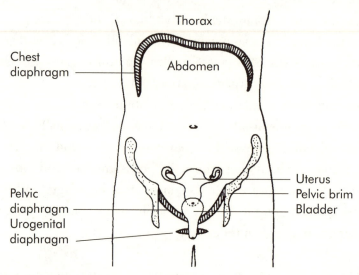

Fig. 2.4. The pelvic and urogenital diaphragms are of great help in increasing chi pressure in the organs. They also work to prevent vital energy from leaking out of the lower openings of the body.

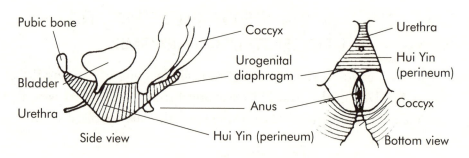

Fig. 2.5. A schematic of the urogenital diaphragm

the pelvic cavity, which contains the large intestine, small intestine, bladder, kidneys, liver, spleen, and pancreas. This lift of the pelvic diaphragm maintains the shapes of the vital organs.

Below the pelvic diaphragm and above the perineum is another muscular diaphragm called the urogenital diaphragm (fig. 2.5). The urogenital diaphragm is penetrated by the urethra; its underside is the attachment site of the root of the penis or vagina. The pudendal nerve connects the muscles of the urogenital diaphragm with the penis or vagina and the anus. A membranous superficial fascia attaches to the back of this lowermost diaphragm and comes forward to engulf the scrotum or vagina (which also contains muscle), joining with the abdominal wall.

The importance of these anatomical structures will become apparent as you progress in your work in Taoist Yoga, especially in the three levels of Iron Shirt Chi Kung and in Seminal and Ovarian Kung Fu (Sexual Energy Cultivation practices). These pelvic and urogenital diaphragms are of tremendous help in increasing chi pressure in the organs and the abdomen. Knowing how to utilize and control these diaphragms will improve your capabilities in all levels of the Universal Tao practices.

THE IRON SHIRT PACKING PROCESS

Packing Process Breathing is the most important breathing technique to master in the practice of Iron Shirt. It is used in all of the Iron Shirt postures, and practicing it well now will aid you greatly in benefiting from the postures.

Packing Process Breathing creates air pressure in a small space so that the body can internalize more pounds of chi pressure per square inch. The importance of expanding the abdomen not only to the front but also to all sides has been addressed in the description of abdominal breathing. The same is true in Packing Process Breathing: the expansion of the front, back, and sides of the abdomen occurs proportionally, until the abdominal area becomes round, like a ball.

In watching children breathe you will notice that their abdomens expand and contract—they go round and then they flatten. In chapter 1 we compared this phenomenon to a tire that inflates to a certain PSI—pounds per square inch—in order to support an automobile chassis. Utilizing this same movement of the abdomen, we can store air pressure (chi, or life-force energy) in various parts of the body. When the internal chi pressure drops, all the organs sink downward with the force of gravity and stack on one another, pressing excess weight on each other and placing a greater burden on the pelvic and urogenital diaphragms. Chi pressure helps the organs hold their shape and uplifts the organs into their own positions so that energy can flow more easily. The chi pressure thus serves as an energy charger for the organs.

Taoists believe that the body has several openings: one front door (the sexual organ); one back door (the anus); and the seven openings considered to be the body's windows (two eyes, two ears, two nostrils, and one mouth). It is through these openings that energy can enter or leak out from the body. In the practice of Iron Shirt we learn to seal our bodies to prevent energy leakage and the loss of chi pressure, enabling us to pack, condense, and store energy in our bodies and organs. Pulling up the pelvic and urogenital diaphragms helps to seal the doors of the sexual organ and anus. Turning the attention of your senses down to the navel area will also help to seal the energy.

Packing Process Breathing

We will now learn Packing Process Breathing step by step. Take the time to practice this breathing process until you feel fairly competent with it before moving into the posture work that follows. Read over this Packing Process exercise a few times in order to get a clear understanding of what is involved. It is a beautiful and powerful practice that can bear fruit in quickening your development of experiencing the amazing vital life-force energy, chi. Try it out to see if you can manage the process while staying relaxed and comfortable at the same time. Avoid the macho tendency to be "gung ho," trying to force it and then getting frustrated. Be patient. There is another way to go.

After the presentation of this Packing Process Breathing method, we will provide a simpler alternative set of instructions. Though this "easy way" may take longer in the beginning, in the long run it might save time because it can help you to develop your capacity to stay relaxed. Some may find this alterative approach more suitable; it is still an effective way to pack your Iron Shirt (or Skirt, as the case may be!).

You can proceed with learning the Iron Shirt postures in combination with this soft and gentle, stress-free, meditative Packing Process alternative. Then at some point, if it seems desirable, you could use your skills to master the more quick and powerful Packing Process Breathing method.

Please note: Menstruating women and pregnant women should not engage in any strenuous Iron Shirt breathing practices, such as Reverse Breathing, Energizer Breathing, or pressurized Packing Process Breathing.

☯ Preparation Using Abdominal and Reverse Breathing (Energizer Breathing)

1. To begin this practice, sit at the front edge of your chair. (This is also the best position for practicing the Microcosmic Orbit.) Place your tongue on the roof of your mouth to prevent any leakage of tongue and heart energy. Listen inwardly to your kidneys and breathe inwardly to the lungs. Look inwardly to the liver, and to all of the other organs as well, to seal the senses from the inside.

2. Start with abdominal breathing, the first stage of Energizer Breathing (fig. 2.6a). Inhale slowly but strongly. Keep the chest relaxed as the area of the lower abdomen below the navel and the perineum begins to expand. (Remember: Abdominal and reverse breathing originate from the lower abdomen, approximately $1^1/_2$ inches below the navel.)

3. Now exhale forcefully. As you exhale, flatten the belly toward the spine. Pull the sexual organs upward; feel the expansion at the perineum diminish.

4. Inhale slowly again and allow the abdomen and the perineum to bulge as you do so.

5. Repeat this breathing sequence for 18 rounds, working up in multiples of three to 36 rounds. The purpose of this first part of Packing Process Breathing is to energize the chi. This part of the practice is also called Fanning the Fire.

6. When you feel that you have sunk the chi down toward the navel, exhale so that the abdomen flattens toward the spine (fig. 2.6b). The chest and sternum sink slightly inward and down, pressing and activating the thymus gland. Exhale once more and push the diaphragm downward (fig. 2.6c). Hold for a long moment.

7. Now, keeping the belly flat and the diaphragm lowered, inhale 10 percent of your full capacity to the navel (fig. 2.6d). (Ten percent means a short, small breath.) Then relax the chest and belly, trying to keep the diaphragm lowered.

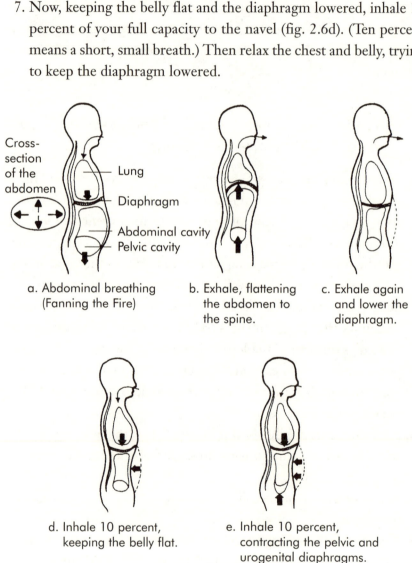

Cross-section of the abdomen

Lung
Diaphragm
Abdominal cavity
Pelvic cavity

a. Abdominal breathing (Fanning the Fire)

b. Exhale, flattening the abdomen to the spine.

c. Exhale again and lower the diaphragm.

d. Inhale 10 percent, keeping the belly flat.

e. Inhale 10 percent, contracting the pelvic and urogenital diaphragms.

Fig. 2.6. Packing Process Breathing

8. Continue with the instructions below, "Building Chi Pressure."

☯ Building Chi Pressure

1. Keeping the belly flat and the diaphragm lowered, inhale another 10 percent while contracting the pelvic and urogenital diaphragms (fig. 2.6e). Pull the sexual organs upward and tighten the anus to seal in your energy. Compress the abdominal organs from three directions: from above, at the lowered diaphragm; from below, at the sexual organs; and from in front, at the abdominal wall. The ribs and spine hold from behind.

2. Inhale another 10 percent. Contract the left side of the anus, bringing the chi to the left kidney; at the same time pull the left abdomen in more toward the spine. Each step of the practice of directing the chi upward from the anus (or lower area) to one or more upper areas in coordination with a small "10 percent" breath is referred to as a "pull up."

3. The process of packing consists of mental, physical, and energetic components. Where the mind goes, chi follows; where the chi goes, the blood follows. The blood delivers fresh oxygen, nitrogen, and nutrients for the cells in the affected area. Therefore, to "pack" you focus your intention and attention on the area of the body you are targeting. Draw the chi up from the appropriate sector of the anus to the intended area for packing with your short 10 percent inhalation. In this instance, draw the chi up from the left side of the anus and pack and wrap the energy around the left kidney and adrenal gland. Contract the surrounding tissues to create the effect of compressing ("packing") the chi into the organ from all sides, intensifying the internal pressure. Then, once the chi is drawn up to and packed into the organ, use the mind/eye/heart power to wrap chi around the organ. Wrapping chi consists of circling chi all around the packed area, as if surrounding it within a fast-spinning cocoon of dynamic energy. You first spin the chi 9 times clockwise, then reverse

directions to wrap the organ with chi 9 times counterclockwise.

4. Pull up the right side of the anus and bring the chi to the right kidney; at the same time pull the right abdomen in more toward the spine. Pack and wrap the energy around the right kidney and adrenal gland (fig. 2.6f).

5. Now both kidneys have been packed and wrapped. Hold this position for as long as you can. Remember: If the diaphragm becomes tight and pushed up, massage the mid-thorax with both hands to

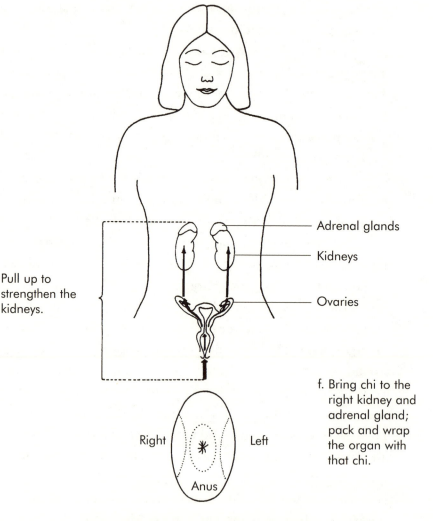

Adrenal glands

Kidneys

Pull up to strengthen the kidneys.

Ovaries

Right   Left

Anus

f. Bring chi to the right kidney and adrenal gland; pack and wrap the organ with that chi.

Fig. 2.6. Packing Process Breathing (cont.)

gently work the diaphragm so that it drops down into a relatively relaxed position.

6. When you can no longer hold your breath, inhale 10 percent more air on top of the air that you have already inhaled. Feel the pressure extend to the area of the Sperm/Ovary Palace (fig. 2.6g). Contract the perineum more tightly, especially the sex organs. You can jerk a little to pack the energy into the lower abdomen, sealing and limiting the energy into a small area. You must maintain a relaxed chest and sink the sternum so that the diaphragm will stay soft and lowered. The abdomen is flat and held in. Pull the sex organs and the anus up again to seal them so that no energy can leak out.

7. Inhale 10 percent more air to the front of the pelvic diaphragm (fig. 2.6h). (You can exhale a little in order to inhale more air.) Contract the front pelvic diaphragm and the lowest part of the abdomen. Hold this position for as long as possible.

8. Inhale 10 percent more air to the perineum (fig. 2.6i). Feel the pressure build in the perineum.

9. By this time it may seem that you cannot possibly breathe in any more air. In order to pack a little more air in, exhale a little and

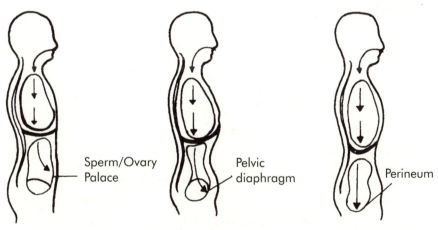

g. Inhale 10 percent down to the lower abdomen.

h. Inhale 10 percent to the front of the pelvic diaphragm and lower abdomen.

i. Inhale 10 percent down to the perineum.

Fig. 2.6. Packing Process Breathing (cont.)

bend forward slowly, directing your attention to the kidneys. Feel the kidneys expand on both sides and backward; this will help to open the sides and back. Relax and trust that the air will have room there and that you will be able to inhale the last 10 percent of your full capacity to that area in the back (fig. 2.6j). Inhale your last 10 percent. Hold as long as possible.

10. Now exhale fully and sit up straight. Normalize your breathing by using abdominal breathing.

11. When you exhale and relax at the end of this session, you will immediately experience heat or feel energy run throughout your body. Lift the tongue to the upper palate. At this point you should meditate and circulate the chi through the Microcosmic Orbit for a few rounds. (If you are unfamiliar with the Microcosmic Orbit practice, see the instructions on pages 58–61.) Collect the energy in the navel when you have finished (fig. 2.6k).

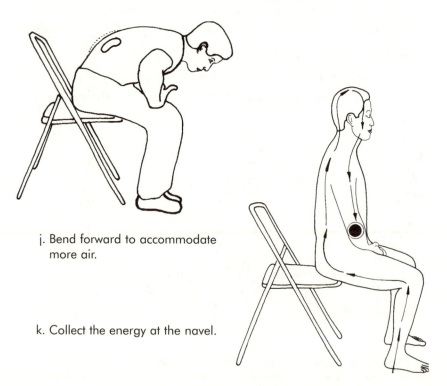

j. Bend forward to accommodate more air.

k. Collect the energy at the navel.

Fig. 2.6. Packing Process Breathing (cont.)

Using Packing Process Breathing the organs are packed, compressed, and strongly massaged. When you harmonize your breath with abdominal breathing, blood and energy (chi) will rush in with great force to clear the organs, making them progressively stronger and healthier.

If you feel energy stuck in the heart area, use both hands to brush the chest in a downward motion. You may also want to make the healing sound for the heart, "Haw-w-w-w-w," and walk around, shaking out the arms and legs.

Points to Remember in Practicing the Breathing Exercises

- Remember: Never use force. Relax the chest so that the chest, sternum, and diaphragm can sink down.
- When packing, stay soft internally; don't tense up. Soft energy is unlimited energy.
- Do no more than 3 rounds of Packing Process Breathing per day for the first week. Gradually increase to 6, 9, and then 18 cycles per day.

An Alternative Method for Chi Packing

Abdominal breathing is the foundation practice for all Chi Kung breathing practices. It is also the basis for the exercise The Easy Way to Pack Your Chi. In order to comfortably and effectively reap the benefits of Packing Process Breathing in combination with Iron Shirt Chi Kung postures, you should practice this gentler, slower, softer version of Packing Process Breathing until you have sufficiently developed your skills in breathing, relaxing, and consciously applying tension and chi pressure to selected areas of your body.

Work with getting comfortable and proficient with the mechanics of abdominal breathing, using the exercise described below, so that the process feels pleasant and easy. Be patient and take as much time as it takes to make abdominal breathing naturally yours. Implement the instructions you've studied up to this point; keep working to improve your technique by using any of the adjunct exercises that follow. It may take weeks or months to undo conditions that have accumulated through years of uneducated habit. Don't worry; just relax and persist with a smile. Things will change.

Stay in tune with the organic nature of the movements for abdominal breathing, letting your intentions blend with the body's natural tendencies to gently strengthen the movement and rhythm wherever and whenever you feel it to be impaired. Enjoy the natural, pleasant simplicity of the life-sustaining synchronicity of movement that is abdominal breathing.

☯ Abdominal Breathing Practice #2

1. Recalling a pleasant feeling, bring the subtle beginnings of a smile to your face. Let a relaxed feeling spread around your face, eyes, scalp, and ears and through your nose and all through your head as you breathe gently in and out through your nose.

2. Let the relaxed feeling spread with your awareness down through your neck and chest and into your lungs.

3. Feel a relaxed expansion and contraction as you breathe in and out of your lungs. Continue to spread your relaxed awareness through your chest, blending your relaxed intention with the natural tendency of the lungs to expand downward in order to open slowly to a deeper breath.

4. Keep the calm, pleasant feeling as you continue your comfortable, slow breathing. Blend your relaxed intention with your awareness of the natural tendency of the diaphragm to lower on the inhale, making a little more room for the lower part of the lungs to expand as you inhale (and thereby absorb more refreshing air).

5. Gently contract the sexual and anal sphincters, closing the "lower gates" to prevent energy leakage. At the same time, lightly pull the perineum area upward to contain the gentle chi pressure in

the lower abdominal area, all the while maintaining your relaxed, smiling awareness.

6. Stay comfortable with the pleasant, smiling feeling as you let the belly expand outward to front, sides, and back, in response to the expanding downward movement of the lungs and diaphragm.

7. When the inhalation has come to a satisfying fullness, pause momentarily and savor the refreshing expansion.

8. Maintain your relaxed awareness as you slowly exhale. Relax the expanded abdominal musculature, allowing the abdomen to flatten back toward the spine and pull the sexual organs back and upward. Enjoy the relaxing release as the extended tissues gently contract to their comfortable resting positions.

9. Feel the complete release of the extra pressure that you may have extended to help the diaphragm to lower. Feel the diaphragm recede upward into its relaxed dome-shape within the lower chest. At the same time, let your sternum sink slightly inward in the chest as the mid and upper chest relax down. This gentle, natural movement prevents the abdominal chi from releasing upward to the heart area (which causes congestion); this movement also presses and activates the thymus gland, and important player in the workings of the immune system.

10. Continue with this abdominal breathing practice until the process feels perfectly natural to you. When you reach that point, continue with the instructions below, The Easy Way to Pack Your Chi.

◔ The Easy Way to Pack Your Chi

When you become comfortable coordinating the combined movements for the inhaling phase and the exhaling phase in a relaxed, slow, deep abdominal breathing rhythm, you are ready to learn The Easy Way to Pack Your Chi. Use the same points as in the Packing Process Breathing instructions Building Chi Pressure (see pages 37–40).

1. Focus your attention on the left kidney and adrenal gland.

2. With your relaxed intention guiding your breath, inhale your abdominal breath to the left kidney.

3. Hold your breath at that point and gently squeeze, using your intention and a light contraction. Hold for 2 to 5 seconds.

4. Release the breath and the tissues. Relax.

5. Repeat at the same point 5 to 15 times, then move to the right kidney and adrenal gland.

You can use this gentler Packing Process Breathing approach for learning all of the Iron Shirt postures in this book.

 ## Adjunct Exercises

The following exercises will be helpful to you in the practice of Iron Shirt Chi Kung. All exercises should be performed in multiples of three as often as the body finds necessary.

Massaging the Diaphragm

Many people have very tight, stiff diaphragms that stick to the rib cage. To release the diaphragm you can massage under the rib cage: massage along the rib cage from the center to both sides; use the index, third, and fourth fingers to push downward from the rib cage (fig. 2.7). Feel the elasticity of the diaphragm. When the diaphragm is stretched your breathing will become easier and deeper. This massage is easy to do in the morning, when you rise.

The diaphragm is lowered during Packing Process Breathing—this is the most important part of Iron Shirt practice. Keeping the diaphragm lowered during Packing Process Breathing prevents the chi from congesting the lungs and heart and allows the chi to continue its course downward to the navel.

You have to be relaxed in order to be successful in keeping the diaphragm lowered. Here's a way to check the positioning of the diaphragm.

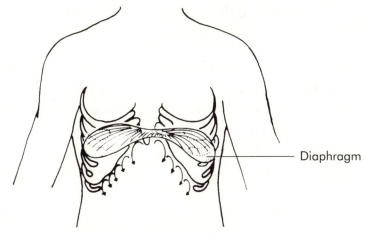

Fig. 2.7. To release tension in the diaphragm, press in and
down all along the edge of the rib cage.

First, with the diaphragm in a resting position, use the fingers of
one hand to press deeply into the point directly below the sternum.
The sharp sensation you feel indicates that you are pressing on the
stomach. Now, keeping your fingers at the same point, inhale and let
the abdomen expand. This time touch the diaphragm under the rib
cage near the sternum, above the stomach. You will feel a sensation
that is quite different from the one you elicited with the first touch.
You will feel the lowering movement of the diaphragm as the abdomen expands outward. There is now a wall of dense tissue that was
not there before. It is solid and you cannot push in as you did before.
That is the diaphragm.

During normal, relaxed breathing, the diaphragm recedes upward
into the rib cage. Chi Kung students have to make a conscious effort
to press the diaphragm downward onto the abdominal area, syn-
chronized with the outward expansion of the front and side walls
of the abdominal muscles. This might be a challenge for extremely
overweight people because they have probably become habituated
to breathing off the top of their lungs due to excess fat blocking the
downward movement in the upper abdominal area. All the more reason to do these exercises: to burn off the fat and to save one's heart!

☯ *Abdominal Breathing in a Lying Position*

Your greatest reservoir of chi is in the area of the navel. Concentrating on this area can increase chi pressure and stimulate chi flow. Your chi always travels to where your attention and activity is centered. When you breathe high in the chest your chi goes there; but because chi cannot be stored in the chest, you will begin to feel distress. Abdominal breathing will negate this problem.

The following exercise will help you to learn abdominal breathing.

1. Lie on your back with your legs flat on the floor, or with the feet on the floor and the knees bent just enough to allow the low back to flatten against the floor. Place one hand on the sternum and the other hand on the lower abdomen.
2. As you inhale, allow the belly to swell enough to raise the hand that you have resting on it, while the chest remains comparatively still. Inhale to a count of nine.
3. Now bring your arms to your sides and exhale.
4. Repeat for 9 more such cycles, this time without the aid of your hands.
5. Now place your hands on your chest and lower the abdomen again and repeat the exercise. Be alert to the breathing process. Put the hands at the sides of the body as you exhale and recognize what you have learned.

Repeat this exercise lying on one side and then the other. To give you stability in this position, bend your knees as if you were sitting in a chair. As you breathe, feel the air expand from the lower lungs to the middle, the left side, the right side, and up, until the chest feels like an air-filled cylinder.

☯ *Abdominal Breathing on a Slant Board*

This exercise will greatly increase the strength of the abdomen and the diaphragm.

1. Lie on a slant board with the head toward the floor while doing the abdominal breathing exercise outlined above.
2. Place a 1- or 2-pound weight on the lower abdomen, then breathe in so that the weight rises as the diaphragm lowers.
3. Now exhale. The diaphragm should go back to its normal position, allowing the belly to flatten and lowering the weight.

Practice this exercise daily, increasing the weight by 1- or 2-pound increments once a week until you reach 10 pounds, or whatever weight you need for developing strength and control of the muscles. You will strengthen the abdominal muscles and soon acquire great control in directing chi to the lower abdomen. By positioning the board higher up on the wall you can increase the demands made on the abdomen and diaphragm.

Always repeat this exercise in multiples of three, working up to 36 breath cycles. When you are proficient at abdominal breathing you can go on to the next exercise.

☯ *Strengthening the Abdomen through Counter Pressure*

The abdomen (tan tien) is the major chi-storage area of the body and the kidneys function as chief regulators of chi distribution. The conditioning from this exercise will result in strong kidneys and a robust tan tien. Strengthening this primary energy center provides the power for circulating chi through the Microcosmic Orbit.

For this exercise you will need a partner who will exert pressure on specific points of your body using his or her fist. Your partner should coordinate with you to determine the correct amount of pressure required for you to respond.

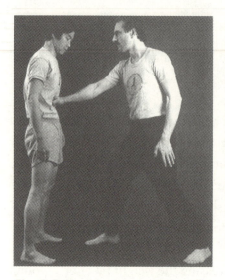

Fig. 2.8. Your partner presses a fist   Fig. 2.9. Your partner presses a fist
against your solar plexus.   against your navel.

1. Have your partner hold a fist against your solar plexus (fig. 2.8). As you inhale, direct your attention and your diaphragm to the point of contact to produce a counter pressure. Practice this 6 times only, resting after each time. You will see how quickly your diaphragm has learned to respond.

2. Now have your partner hold a fist against your navel area (fig. 2.9). As you inhale, direct your attention and your diaphragm to the point of contact to produce a counter pressure. Practice at this spot 6 times, resting after each time.

3. Next, instruct your partner to hold a fist against the lower abdominal area, 1¹/₂ inches below the navel. Inhale as you direct your attention and your diaphragm to this area, producing a counter pressure. Practice this exercise 6 times, again resting after each time.

4. Finally, ask your partner to hold his hand against your side, a little toward the back, in the kidney area (fig. 2.10). (The kidneys are vulnerable and are easily hurt by a blow.) Inhale, directing your attention to this spot to produce a counter pressure. Practice 6

Fig. 2.10. Your partner presses with a hand against your side, toward the back, in the kidney area.

times on each side, remembering to rest after each time. This exercise will begin to strengthen the kidneys.

The effects of this simple exercise are widespread. It is invigorating, it will mobilize an otherwise lax abdomen, and it can help you circulate the chi through the Microcosmic Orbit quickly and efficiently. If you do not have a partner with whom to practice, use a wooden dowel affixed to a flat board. The dowel should be about $1^1/_2$ inches in diameter. Simply place the flat surface against a wall and lean against the dowel so that it presses against the appropriate places in the body, then press back to produce a counter pressure.

☯ Abdominal Breathing in a Standing Position

Iron Shirt practices are mostly done in standing positions. It is harder to accomplish abdominal breathing in a standing position; thus, you need to be more relaxed.

As your abdominal breathing improves from practicing in a lying position, you can more easily control your breathing in a standing position. When we stand the fascia carries tension in order to hold the muscles and the organs upright in the field of gravity. This exercise is for strengthening the abdominal fascia. It is a means of acquainting you with the way the mind and body work together and of learning how to bring energy to a fascial area.

1. Stand with the feet shoulder-width apart. Relax the entire body and make sure the diaphragm is lowered.
2. Take a deep abdominal breath, swelling the belly outward. Hold the breath as long as you can comfortably.
3. Exhale. When you feel the need, inhale.

With an inhale and an exhale constituting one round, practice this exercise in multiples of three rounds.

❂ Developing Iron Shirt Protection

With this next exercise you will gradually train your mind to direct and increase the chi pressure, at will, to the upper, middle, and lower abdominal areas and to the left or right kidneys, packing, wrapping, and energizing them. Soon you will be able to direct chi to the adrenal glands, the liver, the spleen, the pancreas, the lungs, the heart, the thymus gland, or the thyroid and parathyroid glands as well.

1. Hold the fingers of your left hand firmly together, with the inside edge facing inward. Hold the hand over your abdominal area. Inhale. Imagine that chi is filling the lower abdomen and that the edge of your fist is exerting 100 pounds of pressure against the abdomen (fig. 2.11). Resist that pressure.
2. Now relax. Exhale.
3. When you feel comfortable working your chi against this imagined pressure, gradually begin to exert real pressure against the

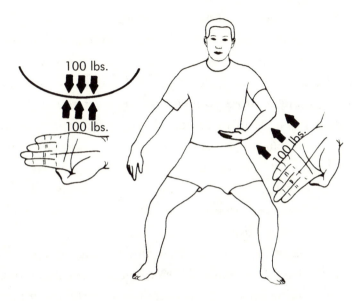

Fig. 2.11. Imagine exerting 100 pounds of pressure
against the abdomen.

abdomen and resist that pressure with your chi. Only bring as
much pressure to bear as the body can handle. Do not force the
energy in any way.

This exercise prepares you so that if you sustained a blow to any
part of the body, you could send chi to that area to cushion the vital
organs from harm.

Most people cannot take a punch to the stomach, which is located
at the level of the solar plexus. But with this training you would be able
to do just that. (However, in the Taoist traditions we do not encourage
people to show off by taking a punch.)

You must make sure that you are relaxed throughout this exercise.
Begin by filling the abdomen with air. You can achieve this by concentrating on the area around and below the navel.

The area from the navel to the sternum is divided into four parts
(fig. 2.12). Wherever you direct your attention, chi appears and protects
the area like an inflated rubber tire. Use no force at any time in this

practice. Simply breathe into the area you want to cushion, and concentrate on it while gradually pushing your palm into it. Do this systematically so that you cover all the body surfaces that you can reach.

Once you develop energy in the region between the sternum and the navel sufficient to protect you against unexpected injury, the rest of the abdomen is more easily protected. The counter pressure that is created drives chi into the fasciae. When the deep fascia fills with chi pressure, the chi pressure will spread out to the second layer of the fascia. (For more detailed information regarding fascia, see chapter 7.) Soon, as you increase pressure in the abdomen, you will be able to move the chi pressure around the abdominal area.

Practice this refinement exercise continuously, in conjunction with all of the Iron Shirt exercises. Once you have become proficient at this exercise using your hand, you can use a short stick in place of your hand. Press the stick into the abdominal area, bringing chi pressure to the area to counteract the pressure from the stick.

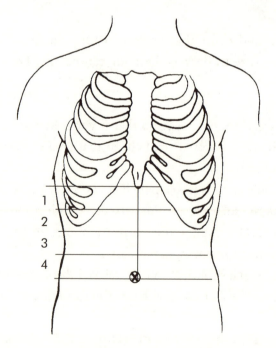

Fig. 2.12. Four divisions of the abdomen between
the navel and the sternum

Summary: Iron Shirt Packing Process Breathing

The breathing processes explained in this chapter are vital to the Iron Shirt practices. Practice Packing Process Breathing until you feel proficient at it before moving on to learning the Iron Shirt Chi Kung postures. Or, as an alternative, you can develop your abilities to feel and augment the organic rhythm of abdominal breathing as outlined in the exercise The Easy Way to Pack Your Chi (see pages 43–44). Then use this gentler breath approach for practicing the Iron Shirt Chi Kung postures.

The guidance of a qualified teacher can be invaluable in helping you make progress with these practices. *Please remember that menstruating women and pregnant women should not engage in strenuous Iron Shirt breathing practices.*

1. Begin with abdominal breathing, expanding the lower abdomen.
2. When you have brought the chi down to the navel, begin reverse breathing with an exhalation, flattening the abdomen. When inhaling, relax the chest and maintain a flattened belly.
3. Now lower the diaphragm upon exhalation while keeping the chest relaxed and the belly flat. Feel the pull of the pelvic and urogenital diaphragms and sexual organs.
4. Begin Packing Process Breathing with a small (10 percent) inhalation. Contract the pelvic and urogenital diaphragms as you simultaneously pull the anus up slightly and pull up the testicles or contract the vagina, closing the lower gates to seal in your energy. Compress the abdominal organs from above, below, and at the abdominal wall.
5. Inhale 10 percent. Contract the left side of the anus as you draw the chi to the left kidney and adrenal gland, packing and wrapping the organ with chi.
6. Inhale another 10 percent. Contract the right side of the anus as you draw the chi to the right kidney and adrenal gland, packing and wrapping the organ with chi.

7. Inhale another 10 percent. Pack the energy into the lower abdomen.
8. Inhale 10 percent more, directing the air to the front of the pelvic diaphragm.
9. Inhale 10 percent more to the perineum.
10. Inhale a final 10 percent. Bend forward slowly, filling out and packing the area of the kidneys.
11. Exhale and relax. Circulate the chi through the Microcosmic Orbit. Finish by collecting the energy at the navel.

Summary: Adjunct Exercises to Improve Abdominal Breathing

Use the adjunct exercises to improve your abdominal breathing and to strengthen the abdomen and diaphragm.

Abdominal Breathing in a Lying Position

1. Lie supine, legs extended or knees bent, one hand on the sternum and the other on the belly. Inhale to a count of nine. Exhale.
2. Repeat 9 times with your arms at your sides.
3. Repeat the two exercises above lying on your side with knees flexed. Make sure to do the exercises on both sides.

Abdominal Breathing on a Slant Board

1. On a slant board, using a weight on the belly, inhale, raising the weight. Hold.
2. Exhale, lowering the weight.
3. Repeat, adding to the weight on a weekly basis. Repeat the exercise in multiples of three for a total of 9, 18, or 36 repetitions.

Strengthening through Counter Pressure

Use mind and body to direct pressure from within against an outside force, concentrating chi in a particular area of fascia.

Abdominal Breathing in a Standing Position

1. Stand with your feet shoulder-width apart. Inhale and hold as long as comfortable.
2. Exhale.
3. Repeat in multiples of three.

CHI CIRCULATION AND THE MICROCOSMIC ORBIT

In the preceding text we have made reference to circulating chi through the Microcosmic Orbit. Your life-force energy must be circulated efficiently and safely through specific pathways in the body in order to be used for healing and growth.

Contained and protected within your spinal column and skull is the very "heart" of the nervous system: the brain and spinal cord. Cushioning these vital organs is the cerebrospinal fluid—*cerebro* meaning "head" and *spinal* in reference to the vertebrae. This fluid, described by the Taoists in ancient times, is circulated by two pumps. One is in the sacrum and is known as the sacral pump; the other is in the region of the upper neck and head and is known as the cranial pump. People who have been able to sense these pumps in action during Packing Process Breathing have reported feeling a "big bubble" of energy travel up the spine.

The Sacral Pump

The sacrum consists of five bones that fuse into one in the course of our development (fig. 2.13). Taoists regard the sacrum as a pump that helps hold the sexual energy coming from the sperm/ovaries and

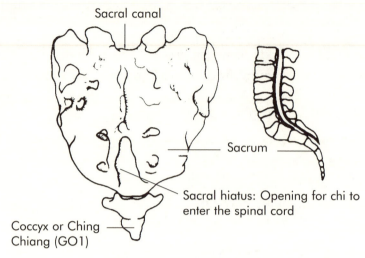

Sacral canal

Sacrum

Sacral hiatus: Opening for chi to
enter the spinal cord

Coccyx or Ching
Chiang (GO1)

Fig. 2.13. The sacral pump

perineum. The energy is transformed within the sacral pump and is given an upward thrust as the cerebrospinal fluid circulates throughout the spinal column.

The sacral pump is similar to a way station, refining the sperm/ovaries' energy as it circulates in the body. In the Iron Shirt practice we tilt the sacrum to the back, or press it against a wall, exerting force to straighten the sacrum. This helps to activate the sacral pump.

The Cranial Pump

There are various energy centers around the Microcosmic Orbit pathway of chi (energy) flow. These "centers" are locations where the chi naturally accumulates; some of those locations are major chi-pumping sites and others are mini-pump sites. The lower centers are located in the lower body and the higher centers are in the upper body.

The cranium has long been regarded by Taoists as a major pump for circulating energy from the lower centers to the higher centers. Medical research has confirmed that minute movements of the joints of the cranial bones occur during breathing (fig. 2.14). Cranial movement is responsible for the production of the cerebrospinal fluid, the fluid surrounding the brain and spinal cord that is necessary for normal brain, nerve, and energy patterns in the entire body.

Improper cranial movement, or cranial respiration, develops for many reasons, often in conjunction with misalignment of the bones of the skull. Such misalignment can occur at birth. When the baby is in utero the skull is soft and moveable; the journey down the birth canal can jam a baby's skull. A misalignment of the bones of the skull may also result from a difficult birth in which forceps are used to pull the baby from the birth canal. Misalignment can also occur later in life, usually from a blow to the head. Auto accidents are often the cause of cranial misalignments. Since these cranial faults affect the flow of the cerebrospinal fluid and thus the body's brain, nerve, and energy patterns, symptoms can develop at any place in the body. Aligning and strengthening the cranial joints can increase energy and alleviate symptoms, such as headaches, sinus problems, visual disturbances, and neck problems. A craniosacral therapist or an osteopath can assist with this realigning process.

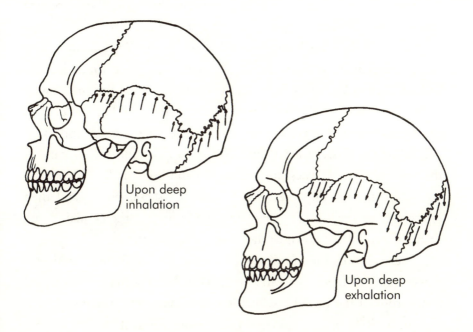

Fig. 2.14. Micromovement of the cranial bones

In Taoism, cultivating movement at the pelvis, perineum, urogenital diaphragm, anus, and the sacrum and cranial pumps is important in helping to move the life force and sexual energies up to the higher center, specifically to the brain and the endocrine glands in the head. The Iron Shirt Chi Kung Packing Process activates the cranial and sacral pumps using various methods, such as mind control, muscle action, clenching the teeth, tightening the neck, and pressing the tongue to the palate. All of these methods will help to activate the cranial bones.

THE MICROCOSMIC ORBIT

The Microcosmic Orbit meditation uses the power of the mind to help activate the sacral and cranial pumps.

It is much easier to cultivate your energy if you first understand the major paths of energy circulation in the body. The human nervous system is highly complex; it is capable of directing energy wherever energy is needed. The ancient Taoist masters discovered that, while there are many channels of energy flow in the body, there are two energy channels that carry an especially strong current. One of those channels is called the Functional Channel or the Yin Channel. The Functional Channel begins at the perineum, the point located at the base of the trunk midway between the testicles/vagina and the anus. It goes up the front of the body, past the sex organs, abdominal organs, heart, and throat, and ends at the tip of the tongue. The second channel, called the Governor Channel or the Yang Channel, also starts at the perineum but it goes up the back of the body. It flows from the perineum upward into the tailbone and the sacral pump, and then progresses up through the spine into the brain and the cranial pump, finally flowing back down to the roof of the mouth.

These two channels form a single circuit, with the tongue acting as a switch that connects the two (fig. 2.15). When the tongue is touched to the roof of the mouth just behind the front teeth, the energy can flow in a circle up the spine and down the front of the body. This vital current of energy circulates in a loop within the central nervous

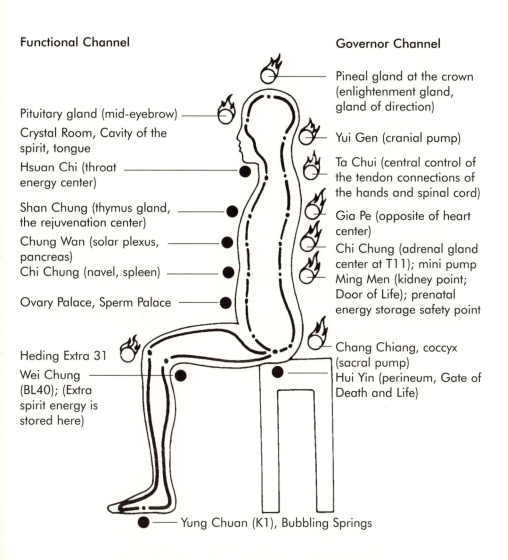

Functional Channel

Pituitary gland (mid-eyebrow)

Crystal Room, Cavity of the spirit, tongue

Hsuan Chi (throat energy center)

Shan Chung (thymus gland, the rejuvenation center)

Chung Wan (solar plexus, pancreas)

Chi Chung (navel, spleen)

Ovary Palace, Sperm Palace

Heding Extra 31

Wei Chung (BL40); (Extra spirit energy is stored here)

Governor Channel

Pineal gland at the crown (enlightenment gland, gland of direction)

Yui Gen (cranial pump)

Ta Chui (central control of the tendon connections of the hands and spinal cord)

Gia Pe (opposite of heart center)

Chi Chung (adrenal gland center at T11); mini pump

Ming Men (kidney point; Door of Life); prenatal energy storage safety point

Chang Chiang, coccyx (sacral pump)

Hui Yin (perineum, Gate of Death and Life)

Yung Chuan (K1), Bubbling Springs

Fig. 2.15. Learn to circulate your chi through the Microcosmic Orbit. The tongue touches the middle of the upper palate to join the Governor and Functional channels.

system and past the major organs, spreading vitality throughout the body and delivering to the cells the juice that is created from organ energy and Inner Smile practices, the juice that is necessary to grow, heal, and function.

The pathway for this circulating energy is the Microcosmic Orbit, the same pathway that forms the basis of acupuncture. Western medical research acknowledges acupuncture to be clinically effective, although scientists admit that they cannot explain why the system works. Taoists, on the other hand, have been studying the subtle energy points in the body for thousands of years and have verified in detail the importance of each channel.

If this circuit is blocked by tension, then learning to initiate the circulation of energy through the Microcosmic Orbit is an important step to opening these blocks. When blocks are present intense pressure builds in the head, taking such forms as headaches, hallucinations, and insomnia. Much of the life-force energy escapes through the eyes, ears, nose, and mouth and is lost. By opening up this Microcosmic Orbit and keeping it clear of physical and mental blockages, it is possible to pump life-force energy up the spine. Circulating energy throughout the Microcosmic Orbit revitalizes all parts of the mind and body.

The Microcosmic Orbit is opened by sitting in meditation for a few minutes each morning as you practice the Inner Smile. An essential Taoist technique described in detail in *Taoist Ways to Transform Stress into Vitality*, the Inner Smile is a means of connecting visual relaxation with concentration. Begin in the eyes and allow your mind to circulate with the energy as it travels down the front of your body through your tongue, throat, chest, and navel and then up the tailbone and spine to the head. Feel the energy circulate through the Microcosmic Orbit by letting your mind flow along with it.

At first when you practice circulating chi through the Microcosmic Orbit it may feel as though nothing is happening, but eventually the current will begin to feel warm in some places as it loops from front to back to front again. The key is simply to relax and try to bring your mind directly into the process, focusing point by point on the part of the loop that the chi is moving through. This is different from visualizing an image inside your head of what that part of the body looks like or is feeling. Do not use your mind as if it were a television picture. Instead, experience the actual chi flow. Relax and let your mind flow with the chi in the physical body along this natural circuit.

Study of the Microcosmic Orbit is recommended to all students who truly seek to master the techniques of Iron Shirt. It is very difficult to progress to higher levels in transforming chi and your creative energy to spiritual energy without first learning to circulate energy through the Microcosmic Orbit. The benefits of Microcosmic Orbit energy circulation extend beyond facilitating the flow of life-force energy and include prevention of aging and the healing of many illnesses, ranging from high blood pressure, insomnia, and headaches to arthritis.

PERINEUM POWER

In Iron Shirt practice we will utilize Perineum Power to direct chi to the organs, glands, and regions of the body that we wish to energize in order to pack and increase the chi in that region. Perineum Power will be used in all Iron Shirt positions.

The perineum region (Hui Yin) includes the anus and the sexual organs. The various sections of the anus region are closely linked with the chi of the organs. The Chinese term Hui Yin refers to the collection point for all the Yin energy, or the lowest abdominal energy collection point. It is also known as the Gate of Death and Life. This point lies between the two main gates: the front gate is the sexual organ, which is the big life-force opening; the second gate, or back gate, is the anus. Life-force energy can easily leak out from these gates and deplete the organs. We learn to seal these gates through muscular toning. In the Universal Tao practices, especially in the Sexual Energy Cultivation practices and in Iron Shirt, the perineum's ability to tighten and to draw the life force back up the spine is highly utilized. Without this Perineum Power our life force and sexual energies can become "rivers of no return."

The anus is divided into five regions: the middle, the front, the back, the left side, and the right side (fig. 2.16). Perineum Power is accomplished by contracting these various regions of the anus, as we do in Packing Process Breathing, bringing more chi to the organs and glands and increasing the effects of the massage that results when we release the tension and pressure and begin harmonizing the breath with abdominal breathing. Toxins and blockages are flushed out of the area of concentration as the chi rushes in along with fresh blood, oxygen, and nutrients. It is a very relaxing, soothing, refreshing massage.

The chi of the middle of the anus is connected with the genitals; the aorta and vena cava; the stomach, heart, thyroid and parathyroids; the pituitary and pineal glands; and the top of the head.

The chi of the front of the anus is connected with the uterus and prostate gland; the bladder, small intestine, and stomach; the thymus; and the front part of the brain.

The chi of the back part of the anus is connected with the sacrum, the lower lumbars, the twelve thoracic vertebrae, the seven cervical vertebrae, and the small brain (the cerebellum).

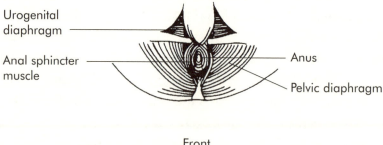

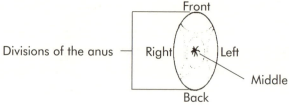

Fig. 2.16. The anus is divided into five regions.

The chi of the left part of the anus is connected with the left ovary, the large intestine, the left kidney and left adrenal gland, the spleen, the left lung, and the left hemisphere of the brain.

The chi of the right part of the anus is connected with the right ovary, the large intestine, the right kidney and adrenal gland, the liver and gall bladder, the right lung, and the right hemisphere of the brain.

The next chapters will teach the chi-condensing and chi-circulating practices and their application to the Iron Shirt postures. *Please heed the following warnings:*

- If you have high blood pressure, check with a doctor before attempting the practice of Iron Shirt Chi Kung. Do not do the exercises and breathing techniques strenuously.
- Women who are menstruating should not engage in Iron Shirt breathing practices. They may practice the structural exercises, standing chi meditation, and Bone Breathing.
- If you are pregnant, do not practice Iron Shirt Packing Breathing; practice only gentle abdominal breathing and standing chi meditation.
- Be sure that the diaphragm is lowered while practicing these exercises to avoid accumulating energy in the heart and to facilitate the flow of the Microcosmic Orbit.
- After practicing the postures, while bringing the energy down to the navel be sure to place the tongue on the roof of the mouth to collect all the energy from the head (the Governor Channel). Take the energy down from the head, slow it down in the solar plexus, and then store it in the navel.

Principles and Practices for Iron Shirt Structural Alignment and Chi Circulation

There is an integral relationship between good structural alignment and strong, unblocked chi flow. The proper practice of Iron Shirt, as well as all other Taoist exercises, will lead to a dramatic improvement in structural integrity and to increased chi flow. A refined understanding of the structural interrelationships of the body is inherent in Iron Shirt Chi Kung.

Because of poor postural habits many people have developed serious structural distortions; they have no natural sense of the proper alignment of the body. If these structural distortions are carried over into Iron Shirt practice, much of the effectiveness of the exercises is lost and bad habits are perpetuated; in effect, such students are practicing the very problems that they need to be correcting.

The following exercise demonstrates how to use a wall to align yourself perfectly in the Iron Shirt Horse Stance, the seminal stance utilized in Embracing the Tree, Holding the Golden Urn, and the

Phoenix postures. These postures will be described fully in this and later chapters.

Whenever you practice your alignment against the wall, when you get to the point at which you feel you can hold the position, step away from the wall and apply the same principles. After you have learned to adopt the correct stance without using a wall, occasionally practice against it again anyway to check yourself. Once you are skilled, occasional use of the wall will allow you to make great strides in your spinal lengthening.

Use this wall position to practice alignment alone; use it also to practice Packing Breathing in various postures. Practicing a full exercise with Packing Breathing while standing against a wall will help to ensure that you can maintain optimal alignment while in the much more dynamic practice of chi circulation.

At first, applying some of the details given in these instructions may seem difficult. However, as your body opens up you will gradually be able to apply each detail easily and naturally. Since these alignment principles apply basic design characteristics of your body structure, you will feel more and more as you practice that your body will naturally fit into these "grooves."

Iron Shirt Horse Stance Using a Wall

1. Stand a few inches away from the wall, the feet shoulder-width apart (fig. 3.1). The feet should be straight along the second toes; the heels are just slightly turned out.
2. The feet are the foundation for your stance. Feel that you firmly contact the ground with the balls of the big toes. Then spread the toes by widening the feet across the balls. Now equalize the weight over the whole foot by balancing the weight between the ball of the large toe, the ball of the last two toes, and the middle of the heel. The toes should remain relaxed and not be grasping the floor.

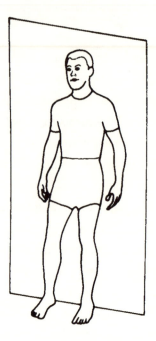

Fig. 3.1. Horse Stance against a wall

As these details become second nature, your practice will be much stronger and you will experience greater body-mind integration. Proper foot alignment is the basis of understanding.

3. The feet should be close enough to the wall so that when your spine is flattened to the wall you do not feel as though you are leaning back. If the wall were suddenly removed you would not need to adjust yourself to keep from falling backward.

4. Practice rooting with the feet. When practicing those exercises that call for strongly grasping the ground with the toes, feel that this clawing begins at the balls of the feet, not at the toes themselves. Accentuate this grasping at the big toe in particular; when you do so your rooting will be much stronger, because the foot is used in a more complete and integrated fashion.

5. Bend the knees so that the kneecaps are directly over the toes. Bend the knees no farther than the end of the big toes. The knees

can be bent less than this, but eventually they should be bent this far to ensure the development of maximum strength.

6. Flatten the lower spine firmly against the wall for as long as you can do so without discomfort. Now place your hands at the crease where the thighs connect to the pelvis. With the lower spine flattened to the wall you will feel the tendon slightly to the inside of the thigh become taut.

7. Tilt the pelvis forward slightly so that the lower spine comes away from the wall. You will feel this tendon relax. You should barely be able to place a flat hand between your lower spine and the wall (fig. 3.2). This will also deepen the crease at the junction of the thigh and pelvis. Continue to feel that the sacrum is stretching the spine down.

Fig. 3.2. Pelvic tilt

8. Now push against the wall at the sacral area while maintaining the other structural details that you have already put in place in your body. As you push your sacrum back to the wall, your spine will arch slightly more and you will feel the muscles around the sacrum become firm. It is very important to feel that you are also lengthening the sacrum further down the wall. If you are doing this properly you will feel a strong force around the sacrum and only a small additional arch in the lower spine.

9. To ensure that this pelvic aligning does not arch the middle spine, maintain the pelvic tilt position. Now gently but firmly push the lower ribs back, simultaneously lifting them slightly higher up the wall. You should be able to feel the middle and lower back lengthen as you do this. This is the work of the psoas muscles.

10. Remain in the pelvic tilt position and bring as much of your upper spine as flat to the wall as possible without straining. Position your head as if it is being gently pushed back from the upper lip and simultaneously lifted by the crown. Again, for many people the head will not touch the wall when held in this way. This is usually due to excessive curvature of the upper spine, which can be eliminated with practice of the Iron Bridge, the Backbend, and Door Hanging. (All of these exercises are described in later chapters.)

11. When chi is brought to the adrenal energy center and packed in the kidney area, it is necessary to lean forward and thrust the T11 area back. (The T11 point is located at the top of the kidneys at the point of the adrenal glands; some find this point easiest to locate by thinking of it as being at the bottom edge of the rib cage, at the spine.) To feel this, simply keep the T11 area firmly pressed against the wall and round the rest of the spine above this point away from the wall, all the while maintaining the other alignment principles. It is possible to feel this thrust very strongly when practicing against the wall, as it is when practicing with a partner pushing at that point.

12. Lift the arms in front of your chest, slightly rounded at the elbows and with fingers pointed toward one another, as if encircling a

beach ball. Then move the shoulder blades firmly back to the wall so that the whole area of each shoulder blade is in firm contact with the wall. Now round the shoulders forward, feeling the shoulder blades move away from the wall until just the spine and, if possible, the area between the inner edges of the shoulder blades remain on the wall. Relax the chest muscles.

13. After rounding the shoulders forward, push back gently at C7, the vertebra at the base of the neck, and at C1, the vertebra at the base of the skull. The chin will tuck in as you do this. Extend up from the crown of the head. Neither C7 nor C1 will touch the wall. Make sure that you don't push back too strongly; you want to ensure that alignment with the upper spine and neck remains correct (fig. 3.3). If done properly, pushing back at C7 after rounding the shoulders forward will increase the rounding of the shoulders, and you will feel that the shoulders have become "locked" in place.

14. Lock the knees and do not move them. As you concentrate on the knees, they will feel as though they are simultaneously being pushed in toward the midline and out to the sides. Now consciously push the knees outward. You will feel a spiraling effect from the knees to the ground, as if your legs were screws being rotated down into the earth. Locking the knees greatly improves strength, stability, and chi flow.

Practice the Horse Stance against a wall until you can feel you are able to hold the position.

Summary: Developing Iron Shirt Horse Stance Basic Alignment

1. Stand a few inches away from the wall with the feet shoulder-width apart. Align each foot.
2. Practice rooting with the feet. "Claw" with the feet by grasping with the balls of the feet first, particularly the balls of the big toes. The toes will then follow in grasping the ground.

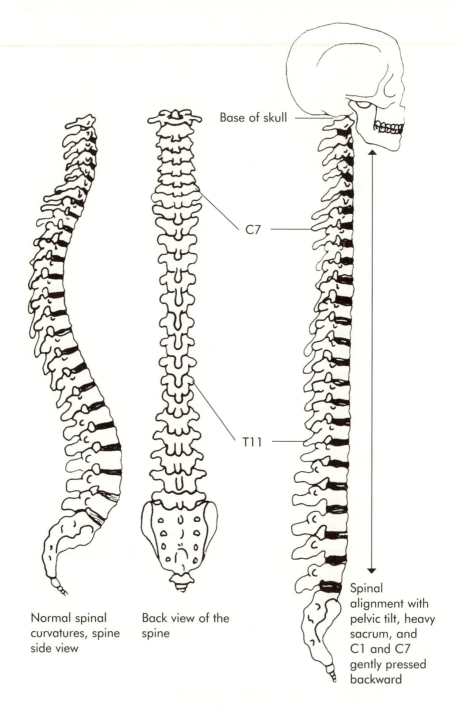

Base of skull

C7

T11

Spinal alignment with pelvic tilt, heavy sacrum, and C1 and C7 gently pressed backward

Normal spinal curvatures, spine side view

Back view of the spine

Fig. 3.3. The spine

3. Bend the knees.

4. Lean against the wall with the lower spine flat, if possible.

5. Tilt the pelvis forward until the thigh tendon relaxes. Feel that the sacrum is pulling the spine down.

6. Push your sacrum back to the wall, continuing to feel that the sacrum is pulling the spine down. Feel the muscles around the sacrum push firmly against the wall.

7. Bring the lower ribs firmly to the back wall, then stretch them up slightly higher on the wall.

8. Bring as much of the upper spine as possible flat to the wall, with the head held as if it is pushed back from the upper lip and lifted by its crown. The back of the head may or may not touch the wall.

9. Push the T11 area firmly to the wall as you bring the rest of the upper spine away from the wall.

10. Flatten the shoulder blades to the wall. Lift the arms to shoulder height, as if you were holding a beach ball. Round the shoulders forward, feeling the shoulder blades move away from the wall until only the spine and, if possible, the area between the inner edges of the shoulder blades remains on the wall.

11. Check that the chest muscles are relaxed. The chest will be somewhat depressed.

12. Gently but firmly push back at C7 and at C1. Extend up from the crown of the head. The back of the head does not touch the wall.

13. Lock the knees, then push the knees outward. Feel as though your legs were screws being rotated into the earth.

CONDENSING AND CIRCULATING CHI: "WRAPPING" CHI AT THE BODY'S POWER POINTS

So far we have learned Iron Shirt Packing Process Breathing, the practice that is used for packing chi into the organs and the fascia surrounding the organs, and we have learned Horse Stance, which helps to develop optimal structural alignment, important for unimpeded chi flow. Now we will go into more detail about circulating chi at certain power points in the body.

We will learn the Embracing the Tree posture as the starting point for learning the chi-circulation practices. Embracing the Tree is the opening position for all of the Iron Shirt Chi Kung postures. Embracing the Tree joins many body structures, including tendons and chi channels, together into one system. In the beginning it seems difficult, quite like piecing together a puzzle. However, if you learn this stance by taking one step at a time, practicing each one until you can master it, then when you move on to the next step you will find the previous one easier to achieve. Also, once you have mastered the Horse Stance against a wall you will find it much easier to practice Embracing the Tree.

Once you learn the Embracing the Tree position you can begin to practice the chi-circulation exercises that follow.

Embracing the Tree

I will now describe the positions of Embracing the Tree in step-by-step detail, as physical preparation for the chi-condensing and chi-circulating practices of packing and wrapping. Practice each step as you read the detailed instructions here. Later in the chapter I give a practice sequence that links all of the steps together. It is best to learn each phase of Embracing the Tree and packing and wrapping chi well before attempting to put it all together.

☯ *Preparations*

1. For all Iron Shirt postures, the correct distance between the feet is shoulder-width apart. The classic measure is the length of the lower leg from knee to toes. Beginners may wish to place the feet slightly farther apart, but the standard position yields the quickest results.
2. Rooting is a very important practice in the Universal Tao System.

Rooting begins with the physical practice and builds into a higher, or spiritual, practice. Rooting creates a strong structure upon which to build, like the foundation of a building. To root is to surrender yourself to the pull of gravity while maintaining a structural skeletal alignment that supports the body in an upright posture.

As we begin the physical practice of rooting, it helps to feel how the Kidney 1 point on the soles of the feet, also known as Bubbling Springs, are the points at which Mother Earth's healing energy enters the body. When the soles are open you can feel them "sucking" and making a connection with the ground. This healing energy passes into the body through the soles and will nourish the organs and the glands.

Like the roots of a tree, the feet support the entire structure of the body (figs. 3.4 and 3.5). It is important to distribute your weight solidly and evenly over the whole foot.

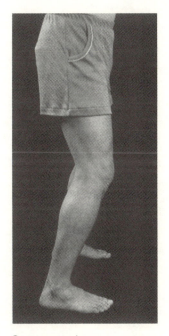

Correct rooting

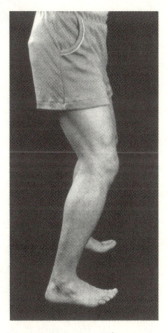

Incorrect rooting—the toes are lifted from the ground

Fig. 3.4. Rooting the feet

Fig. 3.5. Feeling rooted to the Earth

We divide the foot into nine parts, or nine bases (fig. 3.6):

1. the big toe
2. the second toe
3. the third toe
4. the fourth toe
5. the small toe
6. the big ball
7. the small ball
8. the outer edge
9. the heel

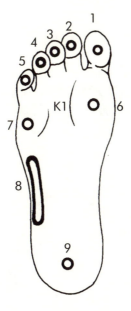

Fig. 3.6. Bubbling Springs (Kidney 1) and the nine points of the foot

You must feel that the nine parts of each foot are evenly contacting the ground. If the toes and ball of the foot were raised, the practitioner could easily be pushed over. Feel and check which parts of the feet are too tense or have too much pressure on them. Tension and pressure can cause the body to misalign and the spine to tilt to one side. Over a long period of time improper alignment can cause spinal cord or disc problems.

The big toe joins with the tendons of the thumb and the little toe joins with the tendons of the pinky finger (figs. 3.7 and 3.8). Thus, all the tendons of the body are connected. You can use this information to increase your rooting power. Slightly pointing the toes inward will help you feel the connection of the big toes and the thumb. In this posture, imagine you have roots extending down into the ground.

At the spiritual level of rooting it is important to know that, as there is a Father Heaven, so there is a Mother Earth. In the spiritual levels of practice many people want to raise themselves to

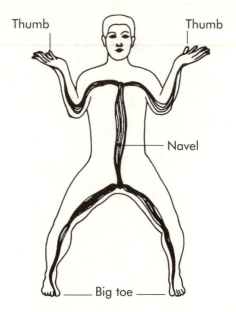

Fig. 3.7. The tendons of the big toes join with the tendons of the thumbs.

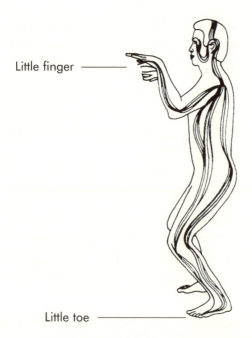

Fig. 3.8. The tendons of the little toes join with the tendons of the little fingers.

a higher level to be filled with spiritual energy. If you want to go higher you must take care that your foundation, your rooting, is good. This connection between heaven and earth is most important in the Taoist practices. In the higher practices the ground energy from Mother Earth is equally important to the spiritual energy from Father Heaven.

3. Abdominal breathing and proper rooting begin to create a feeling of chi as you start to open yourself to the energies of Heaven and Earth. When you feel the chi and fullness down below the navel, slowly sink down into the knees. Feel the sacrum pulling the spine down and the head stretching upward, as if pulled by a string (fig. 3.9). Keep the spine erect. Feeling the spine suspended upward

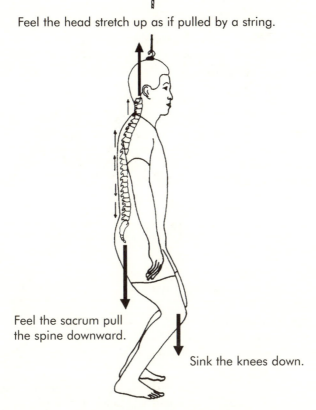

Feel the head stretch up as if pulled by a string.

Feel the sacrum pull the spine downward.

Sink the knees down.

Fig. 3.9. Elongating the spine

and the sacrum pulling downward elongates the spine and opens the spaces between the vertebral discs (fig. 3.10). Gradually you will become taller. This elongation creates more room for the spinal cord and for the cerebrospinal fluid and chi to travel freely.

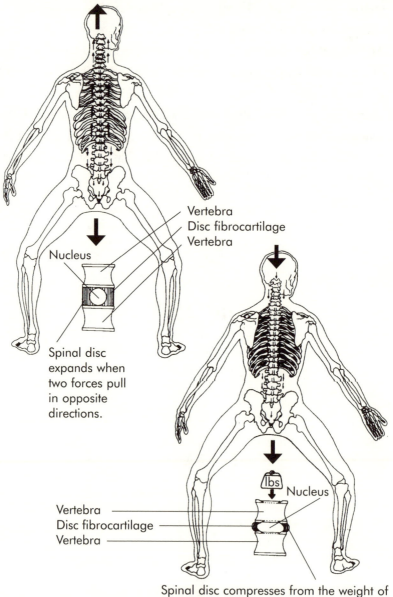

Vertebra
Disc fibrocartilage
Vertebra

Nucleus

Spinal disc
expands when
two forces pull
in opposite
directions.

Vertebra
Disc fibrocartilage
Vertebra

lbs Nucleus

Spinal disc compresses from the weight of
the body unmediated in gravity.

Fig. 3.10. Spinal elongation is healthy for the discs.

Bend the knees and sink your weight toward the ground. Look straight ahead as you step to the side with the left foot to the standard position.

⊘ Make Three Chi Circles

It may be helpful at this point to have an overall view of the Embracing the Tree posture. See figure 3.11.

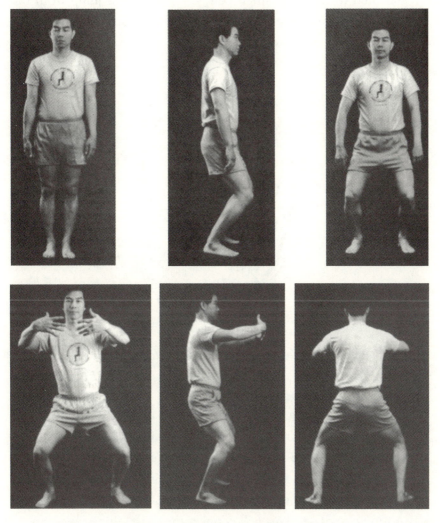

Fig. 3.11. Embracing the Tree posture

1. Now we will work with the upper body. The first chi circle we'll make connects the arms with the scapulae (fig. 3.12). Raise your arms in a circle, as if holding a large ball or a tree lightly between the hands and chest. This forms the first circle. The fingertips of each hand are 1 to 2 inches apart from each other. The seventh cervical vertebra (C7) is the main juncture where energy and the powerful tendons of the body meet. Gradually you will feel chi spreading from C7 to the outside of the arm, to the middle finger, and then to the palm; then you will feel the chi jump from the right middle finger to the left middle finger and from the right thumb to the left thumb.

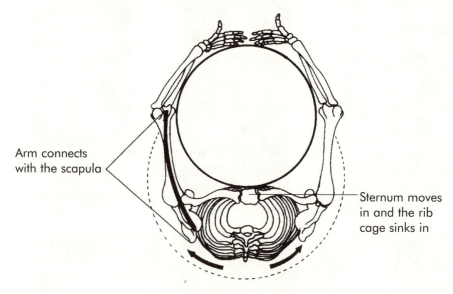

Arm connects with the scapula

Sternum moves in and the rib cage sinks in

Fig. 3.12. The first chi circle connects the arms with the scapulae.

2. The elbows sink down, turning inward; but they should feel as though they are maintaining their position by resisting the downward pull. Imagine that someone is pushing you on the outside of your elbows and you, in turn, are pushing outward to maintain your position. Feel the spiral in your forearm as if it were a screw turning clockwise. This will connect the wrist, elbow, and arm.

3. Relax the shoulders. Drop the neck muscles down. The trapezius muscles, which connect the neck with the shoulders (fig. 3.13), have to be relaxed so that the energy generated by properly aligning the structure can be transmitted downward.

4. Bring your concentration down the spine, pressing down on your skeletal structure to the sacrum, to the knees, and finally down to the feet and the ground. You are pressing down on the skeletal

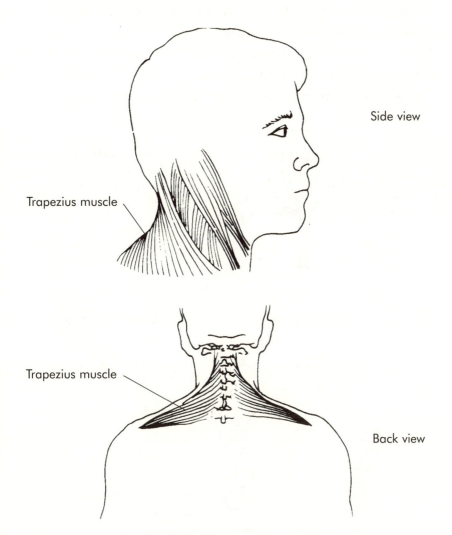

Fig. 3.13. The trapezius muscle

structure to use its support, rather than using the muscles. The pressure gradually travels down the spine to the sacrum and hips, tightening the legs and feet. Eventually you will feel your bone structure connected down to the Earth, rooted as if you had grown into the Earth and were of one piece with the ground (fig. 3.14).

5. Stand tall with knees bent, feeling the weight distributed evenly on the feet. Relax the neck, the shoulders, and the chest. Gradually bring your attention to the navel and send the chi energy to the navel until you feel a warm fullness there.

6. The second circle connects the scapulae with the spine. Point the thumbs upward so that the energy will flow between the two thumbs; this will also connect the thumbs with the big toes

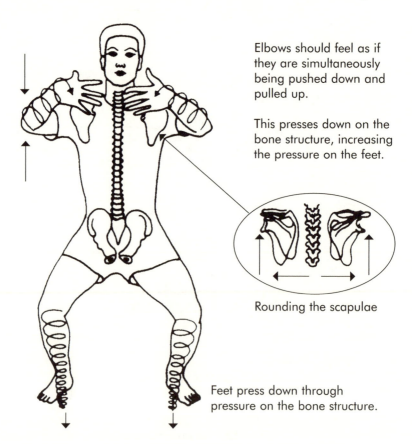

Elbows should feel as if they are simultaneously being pushed down and pulled up.

This presses down on the bone structure, increasing the pressure on the feet.

Rounding the scapulae

Feet press down through pressure on the bone structure.

Fig. 3.14. Press down on the bone structure to use its support.

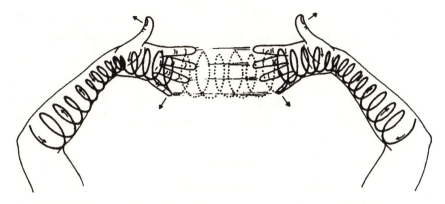

Fig. 3.15. Pull the thumb tendons away from you and the little finger tendons toward you to connect the hands with the scapulae.

through the muscle-tendon meridians. You will feel the bones, tendons, fascia, and muscles of the front body knit the structure together.

7. Connect the hands and fingers with the scapulae and occiput by pulling the thumb tendons away from you and the tendons of the pinky fingers toward you. Feel a clockwise spiraling action as you open the scapulae to the side (fig. 3.15). As in practicing Horse Stance against a wall, feel as though the inner edges of the shoulder blades remain on the wall while the shoulder blades stick to the back of the rib cage. This will transfer force from the shoulder blades to the rib cage, which in turn will transfer to C7—the energy junction point—to the spine, the sacrum, the knees, and down to the feet. In this way the force can also be transferred from the ground to the feet, to the knees, to the hips, to the sacrum, to the spine, to the shoulder blades and, finally, to the hands. Since the shoulder blades, while near the spine, are not connected to the spine, there can be no force transferred from one to the other unless you have opened the chi channels between the shoulder blades and the spine. For further instruction in this see *Chi Self-Massage*.

In practicing this posture you will feel a line of force form, like a bow, between C7 and the thumb. When you sink your elbows and press inward, you will feel more of this bow line. By stretching the scapulae and the tendons along the spine and connecting them in this way, the back becomes rounded and the chest sinks (fig. 3.16). Feel the hollowness at the chest. The sternum sinks down to press the thymus gland, the major gland of rejuvenation and the immune system (fig. 3.17). Keeping this gland active will increase chi flow.

8. These microadjustments will help to activate the cranial pump. Rest and feel the cranium begin to pulsate. Once you get the alignment you will feel energy accumulate in the navel, connecting the chi energy along the front line of the body and joining the boney structure of the rib cage together. By doing this you are helping to sink the energy down into the body.

9. Embracing the Tree will strengthen the thumb and toe muscles

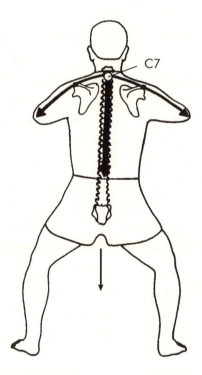

C7

Fig. 3.16. The second chi circle connects the
scapulae with the spine.

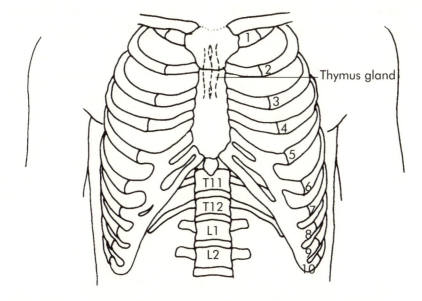

Fig. 3.17. The thymus gland is the major gland of rejuvenation
and the immune system.

and their tendons. The thumbs and toes have the principal rooting power. By strengthening the tendons you are energizing the
muscle-tendon meridians that originate at these points and join at
the navel; in doing this, all the muscles, tendons, bones, and fascia
(connective tissue) will become bound together, greatly improving
the bone structure and assisting you in holding a good posture.
Bad posture is caused by weak tendons, muscles, and fascia, which
cause bones to fall easily out of alignment.

10. The third chi circle connects the hands, scapulae, and spine to the
sacrum. This connection is made by first pushing outward at C7
and T11 and locking the hips (fig. 3.18). This stretches the spine
like a flexed bow and will link the spine, C7, the scapulae, shoulders, arms, elbows, and hands together.

11. Now push the sacrum out as if you were pushing against the wall.
When you separate the sacrum from the ilium in this way and
position the sacrum on a more vertical axis, you activate the sacral

pump, which is crucial for circulating chi. Doing this will make you feel the connection between the spine, the scapulae, and the sacrum. Find and adjust the gravity point of the sacrum in between the feet.

The greatest kinetic energy and power in the human body is generated through the hip joints, around which are attached the

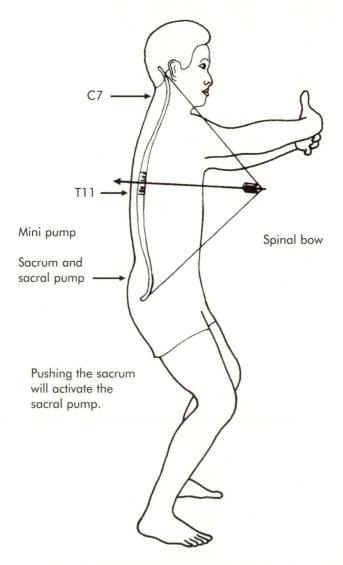

C7

T11

Mini pump

Sacrum and
sacral pump

Spinal bow

Pushing the sacrum
will activate the
sacral pump.

Fig. 3.18. The third chi circle connects hands, scapulae,
and spine to sacrum.

psoas muscles (fig. 3.19). If you cannot open the pelvis and differentiate the two sides of the pelvis, the power of the hip joints is limited to only two directions. The simple act of standing on one leg without leaning to that side requires an internal sense of the angle of the pelvis and the arrangement of the spine. Feeling "empty" on one side can only happen when you feel grounded, supported, and aligned on the other side. (Remember: The interplay of emptiness and fullness is a main principle of the yin-yang relationship.)

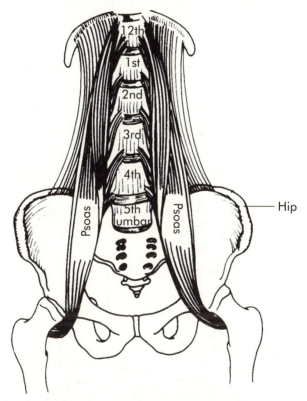

Fig. 3.19 The psoas muscles

12. Round the pelvic area like an arched bow. By turning the big toes inward and the heels slightly outward, the second toes point straight ahead. This will gradually open the groin and allow chi pressure to fill the area.

13. The alignment of the hip joints is synergistically dependent upon two other joint alignments: that of the knees and the ankles. The knees, ankles, and feet are the next connection to the Earth. The proper position for Embracing the Tree requires precisely aligning the knee and ankle joints. The critical point of alignment is where the "saddle" of the tibia (the shin bone) meets the talus (ankle bone), a point that stabilizes everything above.

    To properly position the shin bone over the ankle bone, sink down and open your knees a little bit, turning the knees outward slightly, as if you were sitting in a saddle. Imagine that your legs are screws; feel a spiraling movement downward, as if you were screwing your legs down into the ground. Press firmly on the feet and feel the force of your entire body transfer to the ankles, the feet, and to the ground (fig. 3.20). Feel your bone structure. The knees should feel as though they are simultaneously being pushed

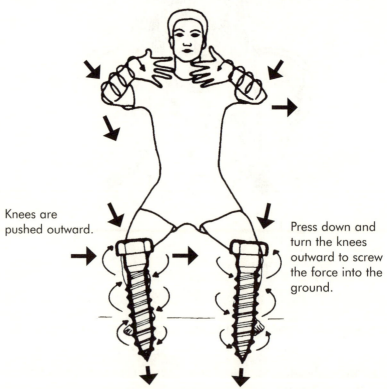

Knees are pushed outward.

Press down and turn the knees outward to screw the force into the ground.

Fig. 3.20. Screw the force into the ground.

in toward the centerline and out to the sides. Lock the kneecaps.

The knee joints should *not* be positioned over the big toes in Embracing the Tree; this causes some people to experience knee pain, making them unable to continue. If you have trouble with your knees while practicing Horse Stance, you must judge just how much Chi Kung you can do. In your own best interest you may have to forego practicing certain of the Iron Shirt Chi Kung positions. Note, however, that the cause of pain does not necessarily lie in the physical location in which the pain is felt.

14. Fold the tongue back to the soft palate, in the area of the Heavenly Pool; if this is difficult, simply touch the tip of the tongue to the gum line behind the front upper teeth (fig. 3.21). Now you should feel the entire body structure connect energetically, from the feet, ankles, knees, hips, sacrum, and spinal cord to the scapulae, arms, elbows, and hands.

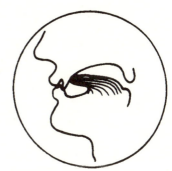

Heavenly Pool   Tongue touches behind the teeth

Fig. 3.21. Tongue positions

15. The Taoists regard the eyes as the windows of the soul, and consider them to be a most powerful tool in directing and absorbing chi into the body. Direct the eyes to look at the fingertips of both hands. Hold the eyes steady to direct the chi flow. Keep the eyes wide open while looking at the fingertips to help connect the chi between the fingers, all the while seeing the tip of your nose with some part of your vision.

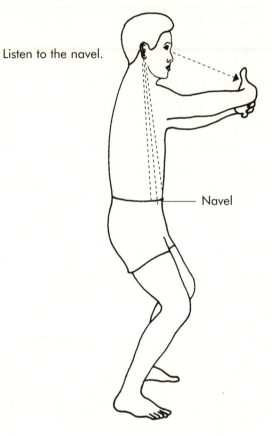

Listen to the navel.

Navel

Fig. 3.22. Centering

16. Listen inside your body, bringing your attention to the navel (fig. 3.22). This focus will make you feel centered, peaceful, and calm.

CIRCULATING THE CHI: "WRAPPING" AND "PACKING" IN IRON SHIRT CHI KUNG

Once you have proper alignment—when you can feel a strong connection with Earth and Heaven and three dynamic spheres in the upper body, all supporting unimpeded chi flow—you are ready to begin learning chi circulation.

Chi circulation, or "wrapping," is the second part of the Iron Shirt Chi Kung Packing Process. When we work with wrapping the energy we are condensing and circulating chi at various points in the body. In later practice you will condense, store, and retrieve the chi from these power stations. These chi power stations are tremendously useful in the Kung Fu energy and spiritual practices.

When we work with wrapping we always begin with the kidneys. The first point of the Kidney Meridian, K1, is on the sole of each foot; the K1 points are the major points for rooting. When the kidneys are strong the bones will be strong, because the kidneys control the bones and the chi in the bones. When you can master the Packing Process at the kidneys—that is, wrapping and packing the chi around the kidneys—you can easily move to wrapping and packing chi at the ovaries, prostate gland, liver, spleen, lungs, heart, and thymus gland.

With the practices taught in the Universal Tao system, I feel it necessary to stress that what you experience is very real. There are no visualizations or acts of the imagination here. You actually feel energy accumulate and then move from place to place in the body because it really does. For some people chi energy takes off on its own; without prior instruction as to where it should be felt, the student finds that the chi goes through the very same routes and stopping-off places that (they later learn) have for millennia been described by Taoist masters. For many students this is a most convincing experience. When this happens they learn firsthand that chi is real and that all one needs to do is to pay attention to it in order to follow or direct it.

There can be a range of sensations associated with chi movement in the body. The most common sensations range from hot or cold to prickling, vibration, numbness, or a combination of any of these, and the same practitioner can experience a variety of sensations across time.

In the beginning it seems that you are very tense and nervous when you practice Iron Shirt, the way you felt when first learning to ride a bicycle. However, once you are trained and know how to move and pack the energy, you will use the body's structure and mind control with confidence, and you will use less muscle.

Preparation: Abdominal Breathing

1. In Embracing the Tree, concentrate on the area 1½ inches below the navel until you feel some chi activity there.
2. When you feel chi activity in this area, begin abdominal breathing. Inhale into the region below the navel. As the diaphragm drops down on the inhale, feel air rush in to the lungs. Feel the lower abdomen and perineum bulge on all sides, like a ball (fig. 3.23).
3. Now forcibly expel the air through your nostrils. With this expulsion of air, feel as though a ball were rolling up your chest. Sink the sternum and press into the thymus gland; at the same time,

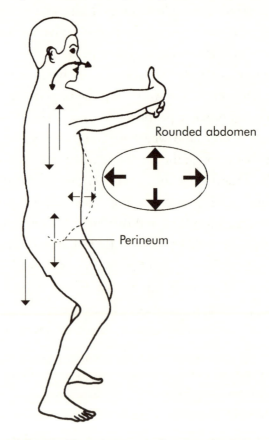

Rounded abdomen

Perineum

Fig. 3.23. Abdominal breathing in Embracing the Tree

pull the sex organs and the anus upward. When exhaling, the abdomen is flat to the spine. One such inhalation and exhalation constitutes a round.

4. Do 9 or 18 rounds of abdominal breathing to energize the navel area and warm up the body. Remember that the breath should be generated from the lower abdomen, $1^{1}/_{2}$ inches below the navel. You can position your hand at the lower abdominal area to make sure your breathing is being generated from there.

5. On your last exhale pull in and up behind the front lower ribs to flatten the abdomen. This will increase and strengthen the psoas muscle. Now, keeping the abdomen flat, inhale once more and relax the diaphragm downward. Gradually you will feel the diaphragm press against the adrenal glands (fig. 3.24). Make sure the muscles of the belly stay relaxed.

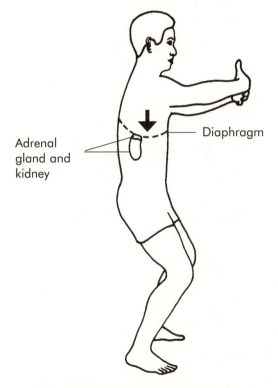

Adrenal gland and kidney

Diaphragm

Fig. 3.24. Relax the diaphragm downward to begin
Packing Process Breathing.

First Stage: Iron Shirt Packing Process

1. Contract the perineum and begin the Iron Shirt Packing Process. Inhale 10 percent of your lung capacity with a short, quick breath, using the navel to pull the air in and to pull the sexual organs upward. (Men pull up the testicles and the penis; women pull up the uterus and squeeze the vagina tight.) Feel pressure build in the upper abdomen (fig. 3.25).

2. Inhale another 10 percent and pull up the left side of the anus. Bring the chi to the left kidney, packing the kidney and adrenal gland with chi. In the beginning you might not feel this, but when you practice for a while you will begin to feel the back rib

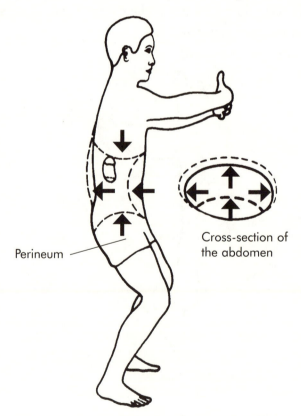

Perineum

Cross-section of the abdomen

Fig. 3.25. Building pressure in the upper abdomen

cage bulge outward as chi is packed into the layers of fascia that surround the kidneys. The sensation is most unusual.

3. Inhale another 10 percent and pull the right side of the anus upward. Bring the chi to the right kidney and adrenal gland (fig. 3.26).

4. Now focus on the navel, the main chi-storage area of the body. Concentrating at the navel center, circle the chi outward 9 times in a clockwise direction to a diameter of 3 inches. Then circle 9 times in a counterclockwise direction back to the navel center. This condenses the chi into a ball of energy, to be finally contained in the navel (fig. 3.27).

Help circulate the energy at the navel by simultaneously moving the eyes in a circle 9 times in each direction (fig. 3.28). To

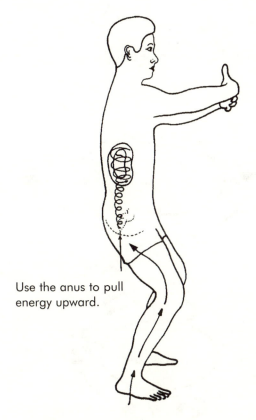

Use the anus to pull energy upward.

Fig. 3.26. Pack chi energy into the kidneys.

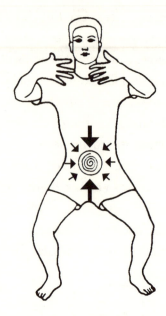

Fig. 3.27. Circling the chi concentrates the energy into a ball.

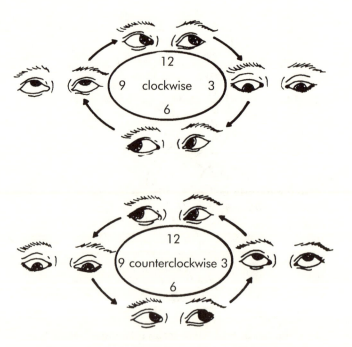

Fig. 3.28. Use the eyes to help make a ball of energy with the chi.

move the eyes clockwise, begin by looking downward and then moving the eyes up to the right corner, then straight up, then to the left corner, and then down again. Move the eyes counterclockwise starting from looking downward, then left, then straight up, then right, and down again.

It is most important to keep the diaphragm lowered during Packing Process practice.

5. Inhale another 10 percent. If you feel that you cannot inhale more air, exhale a bit and then inhale again. Make the abdomen flatter as you draw chi into the lower abdominal area. The area below the navel seems to be filled, but keep the upper abdomen flat in order to minimize the abdominal cavity so that the chi pressure can be increased. The pressure created by the gentle contraction of the muscular outer wall of the abdomen and the diaphragm pushing down from above serves to compress the abdominal organs. Pull up the pelvic and urogenital diaphragms and the sex organs and anus, packing more energy into the lower abdominal area. This is where the chi is condensed into an energy ball. This energy ball will aid in the circulation of blood and lymph through the area, rinsing toxins out of the system and driving excess chi into storage between the fascial layers (fig. 3.29). Remember: the chi will occupy this space, prohibiting fat from being stored here.

6. Inhale 10 percent more of your total lung capacity, pressing the diaphragm even lower and becoming more aware of the contents of the lower abdominal area (fig. 3.30). Women should place their awareness at the area in which the ovaries rest. Hold your breath until the need arises to inhale.

7. Inhale 10 percent more of your capacity to the Hui Yin (the perineum). Pull the perineum upward as you push and pack the chi down to the perineum area, condensing the chi into a ball (fig. 3.30). With practice you will gradually feel the perineum bulge downward. You should be able to feel a channel of chi running from the navel to the abdomen to the perineum. Hold the breath as long as you feel comfortable.

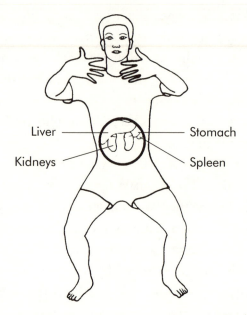

Liver — Stomach
Kidneys — Spleen

Fig. 3.29. Packing and condensing the organs in the abdominal cavity
will increase the circulation of nutrients and
expel toxins from the system.

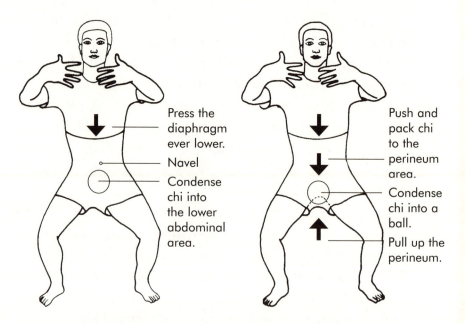

Press the diaphragm ever lower.

Navel

Condense chi into the lower abdominal area.

Push and pack chi to the perineum area.

Condense chi into a ball.

Pull up the perineum.

Fig. 3.30. Packing chi at the perineum

8. Now exhale and relax the whole body, sending energy down the back of the legs into the ground (fig. 3.31). Harmonize your breath with abdominal breathing. When you exhale, pull the perineum upward. Be aware of the middle of the palms of the hands and the middle of the soles of the feet; feel the palms and soles breathing. Coordinate your breath with the palms and soles, inhaling and exhaling with their rhythms—the palms and soles will open easily with Packing Process Breathing. The left eye looks at the left palm, the right eye looks at the right palm (fig. 3.32). Above and between the eyebrows resides the third eye, which Taoists call the Heavenly Eye. Feel the chi from the palms flow to the forehead while the Heavenly Eye sends chi back to the palms.

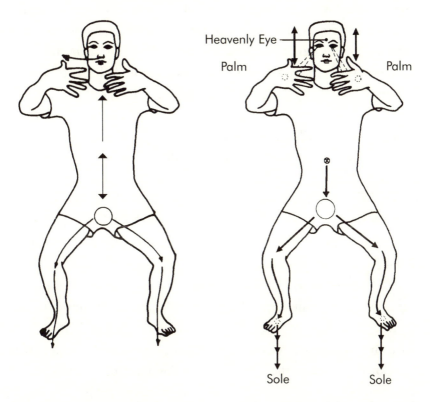

Fig. 3.31. As you exhale, let the energy flow down through the legs and into the ground.

Fig. 3.32. Feel the palms and soles breathing.

9. Continue to feel chi flowing down the backs of the legs to the soles of the feet. Concentrate on the soles until you feel the energy going down into the ground. Gradually increase the energy you are sending to the ground; feel as though you are growing roots downward, inch by inch, like the roots of a tree. Feel the flow of chi from the navel to the perineum, to the backs of the knees, to the soles of the feet, and down into the ground.

When you can feel that you are rooting into the ground, you are hooking up to Mother Earth's inexhaustible sources of energy. Become aware of the loving, healing energy emanating from Mother Earth, which enters through the soles and rises up the front of the legs. Connect with this energy and feel it slowly moving upward until your whole body is filled with this loving, healing energy. To capture some of this healing energy in the body, hold and pack the chi at the perineum until you feel the urge to breathe. Exhale and practice abdominal breathing once more to regulate your breath.

Once you have finished packing chi it is very important to stand or hold yourself still and relax all the muscles of the body. Hold this position for as long as you can, gradually increasing the time. Iron Shirt Chi Kung Packing Breathing creates tremendous chi pressure; you can now use your mind to direct the flow of that chi (fig. 3.33). You will feel the energy flowing throughout the Microcosmic Orbit. Use your mind to direct the energy, from fingertip to fingertip and down the legs and back up.

Each time you finish a stage and are not proceeding to the next stage, you must collect the chi in the navel. Stand up straight, touch the tongue to the palate, and put the palms over the navel. Men should place the right palm over the navel, covering it with the left palm. Women should place the left palm over the navel, covering it with the right palm (fig. 3.34). Concentrate on the navel for a while, feeling the energy that is generated by your Iron Shirt Chi Kung practice. While you are standing practice Bone Breathing, described below.

Practice this first stage of the Iron Shirt Packing Process until you

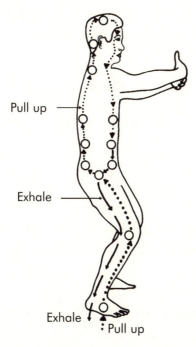

Pull up

Exhale

Exhale

Pull up

Fig. 3.33. Once you finish packing the chi, relax the whole body and direct the chi flow.

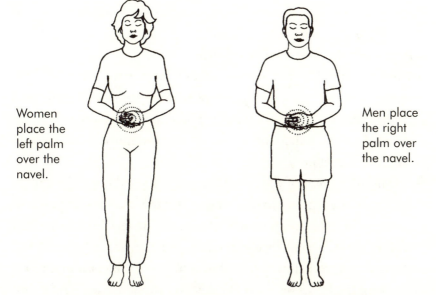

Women place the left palm over the navel.

Men place the right palm over the navel.

Fig. 3.34. Place the palm over the navel and collect the chi.

have mastered moving the chi from the navel to K1 at the soles of the feet and can feel the palms and soles breathing.

 ## Second Stage: Iron Shirt Packing Process

Begin with the first-stage practice as delineated above, then continue as follows.

1. Press the soles of the feet to the floor so that they seem to adhere to the floor by suction. The toes are part of a tendon line and, as such, are part of an energy-flow line. To take advantage of this fact, press all of the toes firmly to the floor—do not allow them to bulge up. When concentrating on the soles, you may find that they grow warm or feel cool.

2. Inhale 10 percent using Packing Process Breathing: as you do, suck Earth energy in through the soles of your feet. Pull the energy up to the sexual organs and the urogenital diaphragm, the pelvic diaphragm, the left and right anus, the kidneys, and the lower diaphragm. Feel as though your soles are sucking the ground. Feel Earth energy begin to enter the soles and move up the leg bones to the knees. Earth energy can feel cool or tingling. Some people experience it as warm.

3. Using your K1 center in the soles of the feet as a hub, circle 9 times clockwise from the middle of K1 outward to a diameter of 3 inches, and then circle 9 times counterclockwise back to K1 (fig. 3.35). Use the mind, coordinating with eye movements, to help circulate the energy.

4. Inhale 10 percent of your total lung capacity and bring the energy up out of the big toes to the knees. Lock the kneecaps and tighten the legs by rotating the knees outward. The feet hold firm. Feel the legs like screws being rotated into the ground (fig. 3.36). Imagine someone pushing the knees in while you resist that force, rotating the knees outward. This action will join the sacrum with the knees and the knees with the ankles and the feet. It also acti-

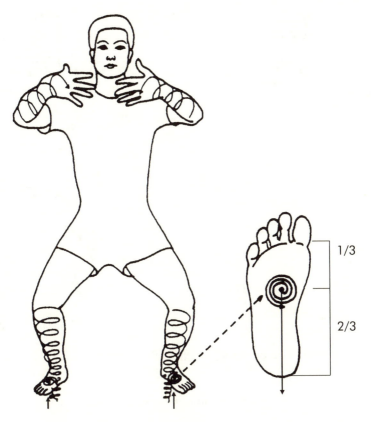

1/3

2/3

Fig. 3.35. Circulate the energy at Kidney 1.

vates and aligns all the tendons of the lower body. Concentrate on the knees until you feel energy collect there. Do not circulate the energy at this point.

When you feel the urge to breathe you can exhale a little bit. The rhythm of exhaling and inhaling is personal; each person must adjust to his or her own needs.

5. Inhale 10 percent as you pull the sexual organs and anus upward, thereby bringing the energy up your knees to the buttocks and then to the perineum (Hui Yin). Feel more Earth energy enter the soles of the feet and rise to the knees and perineum.

6. Inhale another 10 percent and pack more chi in the perineum.

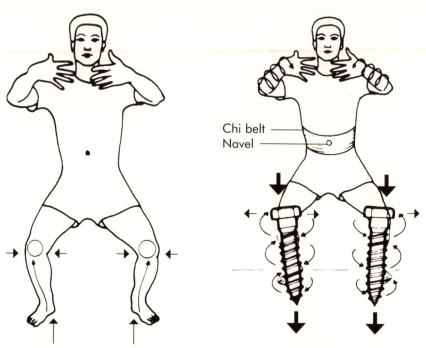

Inhale 10 percent and bring the energy up to the knees. Lock the knees.

Press down and turn the knees outward to screw the force into the ground.

Fig. 3.36. Bringing the energy to the knees

Use your eyes to help circulate the chi energy 9 times clockwise outward from the perineum in a 3-inch diameter and then 9 times counterclockwise back to the perineum (fig. 3.37).

7. Increasingly send energy down to the Hui Yin from the navel and continue to feel energy flow up the legs from the Earth. In time it may seem as though there is a flow, like a stream of water, entering the Hui Yin from above and below, moving up and down as though through a pipe. With this feeling it becomes evident why the K1 points at the soles of the feet are referred to as Bubbling Springs.

8. Exhale. Harmonize the breath with abdominal breathing. Relax and collect loving energy from all of the organs. To create the loving energy you can start your smile in the eyes. Bring that smile down the face, slightly lifting the corner of the mouth, and

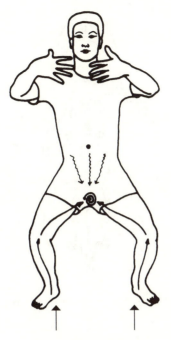

Fig. 3.37. Draw the energy from the Earth and pack and
circulate it in the perineum.

continue smiling inwardly to the organs: the heart, lungs, liver,
pancreas, spleen, kidneys, and sexual organs (fig. 3.38).

Remember that holding yourself still at this point and relaxing
all of the muscles of the body is very important. Feel the energy flow
in the Microcosmic Orbit (fig. 3.39). Remember also that if you are
not proceeding to the next stage you must collect the chi in the navel.
Stand up straight, touch the tongue to the palate, and put the palms
over the navel. Men should place the right palm over the navel, covering it with the left palm. Women should place the left palm over
the navel, covering it with the right palm. Concentrate on the navel
for a while, feeling the energy that is generated by your Iron Shirt
Chi Kung practice. As you are standing, practice Bone Breathing as
described below, then proceed to the next stage.

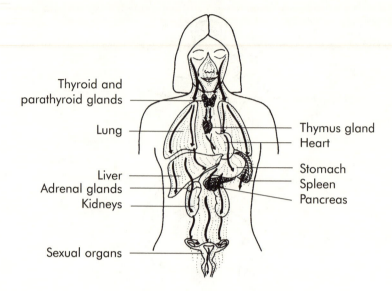

Thyroid and parathyroid glands

Lung

Liver

Adrenal glands

Kidneys

Sexual organs

Thymus gland

Heart

Stomach

Spleen

Pancreas

Fig. 3.38. Smile down to the organs.

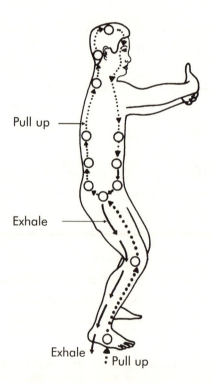

Pull up

Exhale

Exhale

Pull up

Fig. 3.39. Stand still in Embracing the Tree position and feel the energy flow in the Microcosmic Orbit.

Third Stage: Iron Shirt Packing Process

Begin with the first- and second-stage practices as detailed above: Pack chi into the kidneys. Then gather chi at the navel and condense it into a ball, bring that energy to the perineum (Hui Yin), push it to the ground, and then bring it up from the soles to the Hui Yin and mix it with the energy already brought down from the navel. Harmonize the breath, then proceed as follows.

1. After you have harmonized the breath, exhale and flatten the abdomen. Using Packing Process Breathing, inhale 10 percent of your total lung capacity, inhaling up the front and middle of the anus; simultaneously pull up the back part of the anus to direct the chi into the sacrum (fig. 3.40). Put pressure on the sacrum by pressing the soles tightly to the ground and tucking the sacrum without moving the hips. This will activate the sacral pump (fig. 3.41). You can practice by working against a wall, specifically by pressing the sacrum back to touch the wall, as described earlier in this chapter.

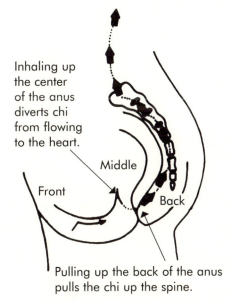

Inhaling up the center of the anus diverts chi from flowing to the heart.

Middle

Front

Back

Pulling up the back of the anus pulls the chi up the spine.

Fig. 3.40. Directing chi into the sacrum

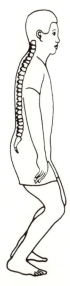

Fig. 3.41. Tilt the sacrum back to activate the sacral pump.

Do not force this move. By gradually strengthening the psoas muscle as well as the muscles and tendons at the hips and sacrum, you will develop a greater range of motion in the sacrum. By activating the sacral pump you increase the volume of spinal fluid circulating through the system and open the sacrum for chi to enter.

2. Bring more kidney energy up from Bubbling Springs (K1) on the soles of the feet to the coccyx and to the sacrum. Inhale, pulling up the left and right anus and the back part of the anus. Pull up toward the coccyx and up to the sacrum, packing chi to the kidneys (fig. 3.42). Feel the area surrounding the kidneys expand as chi is brought to the fascia there.

3. Now circle the energy at the sacrum. Beginning at the center of the sacrum, circle the chi outward 9 times in a clockwise direction

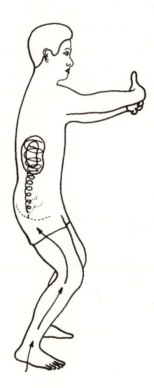

Fig. 3.42. Using the anus to pull energy into the kidneys

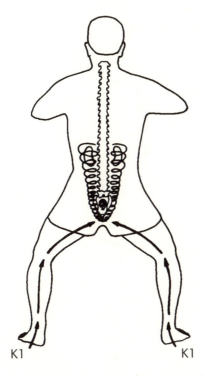

K1   K1

Fig. 3.43. Circulate the energy at the sacrum 9 times clockwise and 9 times counterclockwise.

to a diameter of 3 inches. Then circle 9 times in a counterclockwise direction back to the midpoint of the sacrum, condensing the chi into a ball of energy (fig. 3.43). Use the eyes to help direct the circulation. Feel the chi collect at the sacrum.

4. When you feel the chi in the sacrum, inhale 10 percent and pull the chi up to T11, tilting T11 (and the adrenal glands) back (fig. 3.44). This will straighten the curve of the lower back. Again, use the wall as a guide if you need to. Do not force your spine, but gently ease it until you feel the spine becoming straight. This will open the Door of Life center (L2 and L3) opposite the navel. The pumping action of the sacrum will increase as the spine straightens, and the chi will flow easily, as if through a straight pipe.

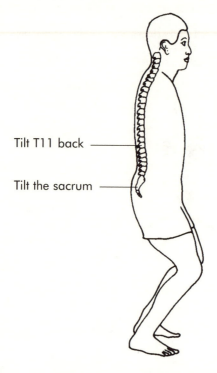

Tilt T11 back

Tilt the sacrum

Fig. 3.44. With the sacrum tilted back, tilt T11 to the back,
straightening the curve of the lower spine.
This further activates the sacral pump.

With the curve of the lower back straightened you will be giving
the psoas muscle a strong stretch. This will help tremendously in
strengthening the lower back.

5. Connect the sacrum and C7—feel the connection between the
   two as a hollow pipe. Now bring the chi to T11. Concentrating at
   this center, circle the chi outward 9 times clockwise to a diameter
   of 3 inches. Then circle 9 times in a counterclockwise direction
   back to that center, finally condensing the chi there (fig. 3.45). It
   can take a while for your practice to develop to the point that you
   can feel the sacrum and T11 fuse into one channel. Be patient and
   diligent in your practice. It will come.

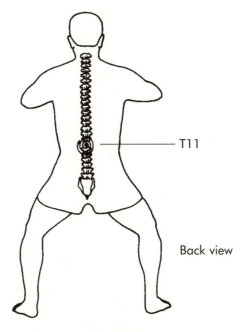

T11

Back view

Fig. 3.45. Circulate the chi at T11 9 times clockwise and
9 times counterclockwise.

6. Inhale and pull the chi from T11 up to C7. Push from the sternum to tilt C7 back (fig. 3.46). Lock the neck by tucking the chin,
clenching the teeth, squeezing the temples and the occipital bone,
and pressing the tongue firmly to the roof of the mouth (fig. 3.47).
This will connect the neck to the spine and sacrum, creating a tension similar to an arched bow (fig. 3.48); it also connects the neck
to the legs and heels.

As the energy moves up from the sacrum to C7, a major push
of internal force occurs. (The seventh cervical vertebra [C7], T11,
and the sacrum are known as the "stations of internal force.")
Once you can feel this force in C7 you will be able to exert it to
activate the cranial pump. Self-activating the cranial pump in this
way greatly increases its action, thereby increasing brain power as
well.

Circle 9 times clockwise and 9 times counterclockwise at C7.

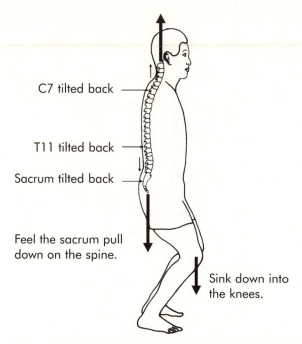

C7 tilted back

T11 tilted back

Sacrum tilted back

Feel the sacrum pull
down on the spine.

Sink down into
the knees.

Fig. 3.46. Pull the chi from T11 up to C7; tilt C7 back.

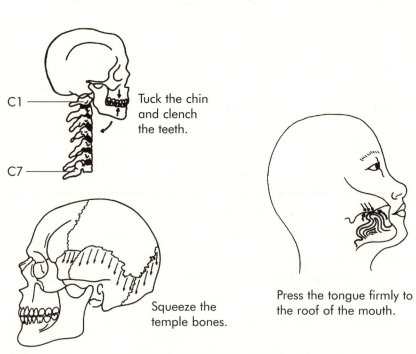

C1

C7

Tuck the chin
and clench
the teeth.

Squeeze the
temple bones.

Press the tongue firmly to
the roof of the mouth.

Fig. 3.47. Locking the head

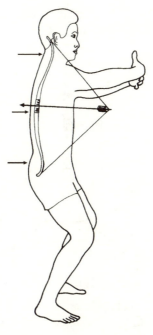

Fig. 3.48. Create a tension similar to a fully arched bow.

Feel the chi energy join the scapulae, the arms, and the hands and fingers. You will feel the chi start to flow from the thumb and fingers of one hand to the thumb and fingers of the other hand, like the action of a jumper cable. Use the eyes to look at the thumbs and direct the chi to that point, bringing chi all the way out to the fingers, moving energy to the furthest reaches of the body.

7. If you feel out of breath, exhale a little bit. Then inhale another 10 percent and bring the chi up to the Yu Chen, C1, circling it 9 times clockwise and 9 times counterclockwise, as you did at the points previously described, until you feel that chi has developed there (fig. 3.49).

8. Take one more short inhale and pull the chi up to the crown, the seat of the pineal gland. Look up between your eyebrows to help pull the chi to the crown. Circle the chi 9 times clockwise and 9

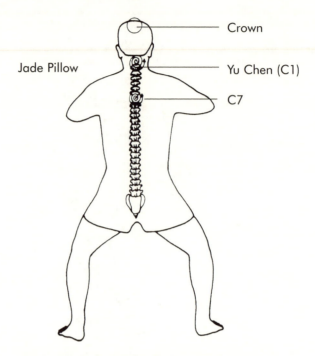

Fig. 3.49. Drawing chi up the cervical spine

times counterclockwise until you feel energy there (fig. 3.50). Feel the energy flow from the sacrum to the Door of Life at L2/L3, to T11, to C7, to C1 and the occipital bone, and to the crown. Feel these points link to one another and fuse into one channel.

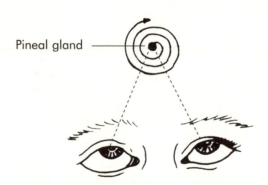

Fig. 3.50. Circulate the energy in the pineal gland.

9. Pull up once again and exhale. Harmonize your breathing with abdominal breathing.

10. Make sure that the tongue is up on the roof of the mouth. Bring the energy down from the crown to the third eye, concentrating there for a while as you practice abdominal breathing and feel the energy build once again. Then bring the energy down to the palate, where the tongue will serve as a switch joining the Governor Channel and the Functional Channel. Bring the chi down to the throat, to the heart center, and then to the solar plexus (Chung Wan, CO12). Circle the energy 9 times clockwise and 9 times counterclockwise at the solar plexus (fig. 3.51). Use the eyes to help in this circulation.

11. Finally, bring the energy to the navel (fig. 3.52). Concentrate there until you can feel chi flowing freely down the Functional Channel to the navel. Listen and look inside.

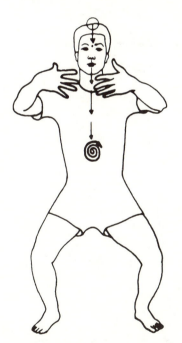

Fig. 3.51. Bringing the energy down the Functional Channel and circulating at the solar plexus

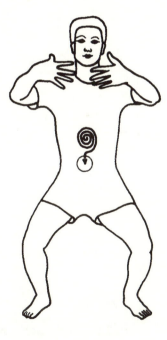

Fig. 3.52. Bringing the energy down to the navel

12. Relax all of the muscles of the body. Feel the chi flowing in one circulating motion to the Microcosmic Orbit: from the navel to the perineum, to the soles, up to the knees, to the perineum again, to the sacrum and up through the spine to the crown, then down to the third eye, to the throat, to the heart, and back to the navel (fig. 3.53). When you feel the circle is moving well, simply let it flow by itself. Feel the navel becoming warm and filling with chi.

Hold this position for as long as possible—simply standing for ten to fifteen minutes and experiencing this powerful energy flow through the Microcosmic Orbit will shorten the time necessary for mastering all of the Iron Shirt techniques. You have created tremendous chi pressure; your mind will condense and direct the flow.

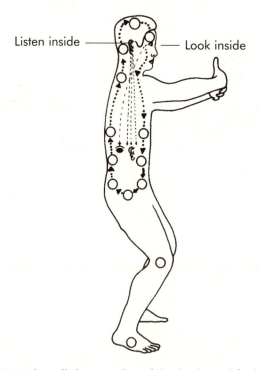

Listen inside ——— ——— Look inside

Fig. 3.53. Relax all the muscles of the body and feel the chi flowing throughout the Microcosmic Orbit.

13. Stand up straight, continuing to touch the tongue to the palate, and put the palms over the navel. Men should place the right palm over the navel, covering it with the left palm. Women should place the left palm over the navel, covering it with the right palm. Concentrate on the navel for a while, feeling the energy that has been generated by these Chi Kung exercises. As you are standing, practice the Bone Breathing Process described below.

BONE BREATHING

The Bone Breathing Process is practiced immediately after you finish condensing and circulating chi in Embracing the Tree, whether you finish your practice at the first stage or go all the way through the third stage.

At this time your body is still filled with energy. Bone Breathing, or bone compression, is a means of using that energy to cleanse the marrow, cleaning out fat in the bone cavity so that you can direct and absorb creative (sexual) energy into the bone to help regrow the bone marrow. We take advantage of the chi we have just generated by absorbing chi into the bones, thereby greatly increasing its circulation. With increased circulation the chi is permitted to flow freely into the bones and the blood, carrying necessary nutrients and oxygen, and is permitted to circulate freely throughout the body. Tension in the muscles surrounding the bones is reduced. The bones become strong and healthy because the marrow, as the major product of red and white blood cells, now has room to grow.

 ### Bone Breathing

Bone Breathing takes time to learn well. It is most important that you relax and are not tense when you practice Bone Breathing.

1. To begin the Bone Breathing Process, use the powers of your mind and your eyes to gradually breathe outside energy in through the

fingertips and toes. Breathe that energy up through the bones to the hands and arms, to the skull, and then down the spinal column and legs (fig. 3.54).

Breathing through the fingertips and toes into each of these body parts will elicit some sensation. Some people report a numbness, others a fullness, still others a tingling or "something different" in their bones. Many people claim to feel more in their legs than in their arms. Feel inside the bones. Bone Breathing is practiced to cleanse the fat stored in the bone marrow to make room for positive energy, such as creative energy (sexual power), which will allow the bones to store, rebuild, and grow the marrow.

2. In the second stage of the practice, inhale through the toes and then, by degrees, inhale up to and into the thigh bones. After inhaling hold your breath, but not so long that you experience discomfort. Then exhale down and out through the toes.

3. Now inhale up through the legs and into the hips, then exhale down and out through the legs.

4. When you have accomplished this, breathe in through the legs to the sacrum. Here you may feel energy surge up through the back and throughout the entire nervous system. Breathe up the back; the breath will be quite long at this point.

5. Finally, while you breathe through the legs and up the back, also breathe in through the fingers, up into the arms and shoulders, through C7, and into the head.

Keep in mind that energy is absorbed and released more effectively when it is directed to specific places, such as the toes, fingertips, elbows, knees, sacrum, C7, the Door of Life, the shoulders, or the tip of the nose. In advanced Chi Kung practices you learn to breathe through the skin to push the chi into the bones and wrap chi around the bones (fig. 3.55).

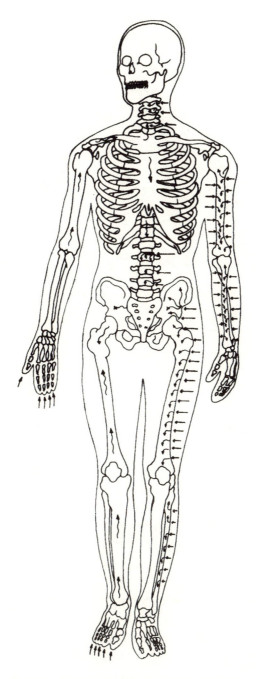

Fig. 3.54. Breathe chi up the arms and legs through the bones, up to the skull, and down the spine and legs.

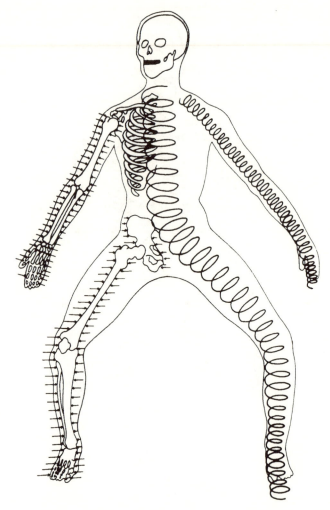

Fig. 3.55. In advanced techniques you learn to breathe through the skin to push the chi into the bones and wrap the chi around the bones.

MUSCLES AND THE EMOTIONS

In this stressful life, pollution and chemicals accumulate in the body, depositing in our organs. In the Universal Tao system we believe that all emotions, negative and positive, are also stored in the organs. When the organs are filled with toxins, sediment, waste materials, and too many negative emotions, these substances will back up into the particular muscle that handles the overflow for each organ. This process works similarly to the manner in which a backup tank works. If we do not squeeze the muscles by condensing and circulating chi, thereby eliminating the undesirable elements and emotions that have been stored there, the muscles will become tense and clamp onto the bones, resulting in stressful feelings that are exhibited in the body and in the emotions.

When the negative emotions are cleaned out of the organs, the positive emotions have more room to grow there. Positive emotions make the muscles relaxed and loose. The Power Exercise, also known as Dynamic Tension, is another means of increasing the flow of chi to the bones and squeezing out toxins, sediment, and waste materials as well as any negative emotions that have become stored in the muscles. This exercise works the body evenly and does not tire the muscles. By practicing the Power Exercise just a few minutes a day you can tone the muscles and help move sediments and waste materials from the muscle tissue (fig. 3.56).

Power Exercise

Practice this exercise from the Embracing the Tree stance, or you can simply continue from the Bone Breathing Process. If you tire in the standing position, rest and walk for a while and then resume from Embracing the Tree.

1. Relax the hand muscles. Now use the mind to tighten the muscles of the hand, and then allow the mind to travel upward to squeeze the muscles of the forearms to the radius and the ulna, the bones of the forearm.
2. Hold the muscles firmly to the bones for 30 to 60 seconds. Exhale strongly through the mouth, then totally relax the muscles and the shoulders. Feel the rush of chi as negative emotions and toxic tensions, such as fear of attack, leave the muscles. Feel positive emotions, such as recognizing the way to proceed; allow the life-force

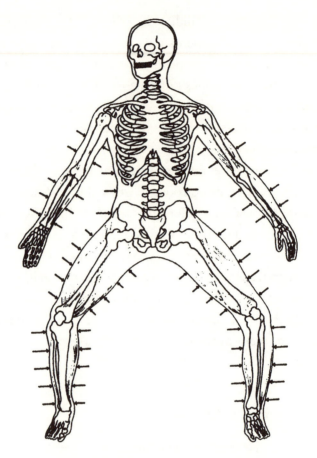

Fig. 3.56. The Power Exercise tones the muscles by compressing muscles and bones.

energy of those positive emotions to enter into the muscles.

3. Relax the arm muscles. Now inhale and spread the muscles of the upper arm into the humerus, the bone of the upper arm.

4. Tighten the muscles all around the upper arm. Hold the muscles tightly to the bone for 30 to 60 seconds. Now exhale and release the muscles. Let go of the fear that you cannot do it. Let go of weakness. Release any feelings of sorrow and loss. Let positive emotions enter into these muscles. Know that you can do this. Feel how strong you are. Feel that you are capable and can take on responsibility.

5. Relax the legs. Now inhale and squeeze the muscles around the fibula and tibia, the bones of the lower leg.

6. Hold the muscles tightly to the bones for 30 to 60 seconds and then exhale. Relax the muscles, letting go of toxins and accumulated negative emotions, such as hesitation and procrastination. Allow positive feelings, such as preparedness or readiness to grow, to enter your being. Be aware of the chi that is generated.

7. Relax the thighs. Now inhale and squeeze the muscles around the femur, the thigh bone. Squeeze the muscles tightly to the bones and hold for 30 to 60 seconds. Then exhale and relax the muscles away from the bones. Release the feeling of lack of support; let the feeling of support grow. Be aware of the chi flowing between the bone and muscle.

8. Relax the neck. Now inhale and squeeze the muscles of the head and neck. Hold the squeeze tightly for 30 to 60 seconds. Relax and let go of guilt and fear. Feel expressiveness, responsiveness, and the willingness to take risks growing inside you.

9. Relax the chest and the back, especially the spinal cord. Inhale and squeeze the muscles around the rib cage and around the spinal cord, from the thoracic vertebrae down to the lumbar vertebrae and the sacrum. Hold for 30 to 60 seconds.

10. Now release the entire spinal cord and the rib cage. Relax and let go of the fear of being taken advantage of or of being cheated. Let go of any feelings of cowardice or the desire to run away. Release sorrow, grief, and tiredness. Grow the positive feelings of bravery, openness, and the ability to take charge and to perform.

11. After you have practiced step by step for a few weeks, you can practice steps 1 through 10 as one movement by squeezing the muscles of the hands, arms, legs, neck and head, chest, and spinal cord simultaneously. Hold the squeeze for 30 to 60 seconds, then release totally. Feel the muscles separate from the bones.

12. When you finish the exercise, stand up straight and put the palm on the navel. Men should put the right hand on the navel, covered by the left palm. Women should place the left hand on the navel,

with the right palm over the left. Stand still for a while and feel how the chi flows. Then concentrate on collecting the energy into the navel.

Starting at the navel, men should spiral the energy outward in a clockwise direction, making 36 revolutions, being careful not to spiral above the diaphragm or below the pubic bone. Circling beyond the pubic bone allows the energy to leak out. Once you have completed the clockwise revolutions, spiral inward in the opposite direction 24 times, ending and collecting the energy at the navel.

Women should make the same action, but begin by spiraling the energy out from the navel 36 times in a counterclockwise direction and spiraling back to the navel 24 times in a clockwise direction.

13. When you are finished, walk around a bit. If you feel the chest tighten or if you feel any congestion, use the palms and gently brush down the chest from the collarbone toward the pubis to bring the chi downward.

Putting It All Together: Embracing the Tree with Chi Condensing and Chi Circulating

The following script encapsulates all of what has been taught in detail earlier in this chapter. When you have practiced well and feel that you understand each part of the previous exercises, you can begin using this script for your Iron Shirt Chi Kung explorations. Use figure 3.57 as a visual guide.

1. Assume a Horse Stance. Sink the upper body down onto the hips, keeping the back straight and positioning the feet shoulder-width apart. Turn the toes slightly inward and the heels slightly outward. The knees are bent and the groin area is relaxed and open.

2. Extend the arms out in front of you at shoulder height. Make your three chi circles, connecting arms with scapulae; the scapulae with the spine; and hands, arms, and scapulae with the sacrum. The palms face you. Gently separate the fingers, thumbs pointing up;

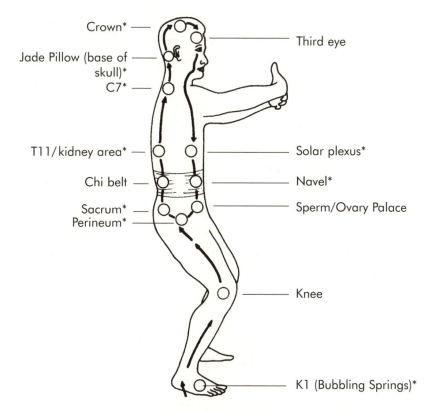

Crown* —

Jade Pillow (base of — skull)*

C7* —

T11/kidney area* —

Chi belt —

Sacrum* —
Perineum* —

Third eye

Solar plexus*

Navel*

Sperm/Ovary Palace

Knee

K1 (Bubbling Springs)*

Fig. 3.57. Points of focus in Embracing the Tree. The asterisks indicate places where the energy is circulated 9 times clockwise and 9 times counterclockwise.

the fingertips are held apart a distance of 1 to 2 inches. Feel as though you are lightly encircling a ball or a tree trunk.

3. Place the tongue on the palate. Breathe in and out deeply 9 or 18 times so that, with each exhale, the abdomen contracts and the thoracic diaphragm lifts up into the chest, compressing the lungs and pulling the sexual organs upward. When you inhale, the thoracic diaphragm expands down to compress the abdomen; at that time you can feel the perineum bulge outward.

4. After 9 or 18 breath cycles, inhale 10 percent of your total oxygen capacity to the level of the navel, keeping the abdomen flat. Press the diaphragm downward. Pull the sexual organs up—for women

this feels like closing the vagina tight—and pull the anus closed. Inhale again and pull up the left and right sides of the anus, bringing chi to the kidneys. Pack and wrap the chi at the kidneys, then circle the energy in the navel 9 times clockwise and 9 times counterclockwise to collect the energy there.

5. Inhale 10 percent of your oxygen capacity down to 3 inches below the navel, to the Ovary Palace for women or the Sperm Palace for men. Pack the chi in this region. Inhale 10 percent more of your capacity down to the perineum and hold that breath as long as you comfortably can. Keep on inhaling and packing in as long as you feel comfortable. Sometimes you can exhale a little bit so that you can inhale more. In the beginning, inhale smaller amounts of oxygen in short periods of time. When you have trained for a while you can hold more air for a longer time.

6. Now exhale and send energy down the backs of the legs into the Earth. The feet will fill with energy. Feel the palms and soles of the feet breathing. Coordinate your breath with their rhythms, inhaling and exhaling through the palms and the soles.

7. Press down through the feet, especially at the big toes. Feel that you are sucking energy up from the Earth through Bubbling Springs, the Kidney 1 point on the soles of the feet. "Claw" the floor with the feet as you inhale and draw the energy out of the ground. Collect chi at the Bubbling Springs points by circling the energy 9 times clockwise and 9 times counterclockwise.

8. Contract the muscles of the anus and groin and pull up the testicles or the vagina. Inhale and bring the energy up the front of the legs to the knees. Hold the chi at the knees and lock the knees by rotating them slightly outward.

9. Bring the energy to the buttocks by turning the thigh muscles (the quadriceps) in toward the midline while keeping the knees turning outward. Bring the energy into the perineum. Hold the chi here and circle it 9 times clockwise and 9 times counterclockwise.

10. Exhale and regulate the breath with 9 or 18 rounds of abdominal breathing, continuing to feel the palms and soles breathe.

11. Inhale 10 percent, pulling up the left and right sides of the anus and packing the back area and kidneys.

12. Contract the back part of the anus as you inhale to bring chi up to the sacrum. Pull up the testicles or the vagina. Put pressure on the sacrum by pressing the soles of the feet to the ground and tucking the sacrum. (Do not tilt the hips as you tuck the sacrum.) Tucking the sacrum pushes the lumbar vertebrae outward and straightens the curves of the spine. Inhale 10 percent of your capacity and pack chi into the sacrum. Collect the energy there by mentally circling it 9 times clockwise and 9 times counterclockwise. Continue to contract the anus.

13. Inhale 10 percent of your capacity again. Pull the chi up to T11, tilting T11 back to straighten the curve of the lower back. Collect the energy at T11 by circling 9 times clockwise and then 9 times counterclockwise.

14. Inhale 10 percent of your capacity and pack more chi into the whole region of the back. Continue to tighten the anus and groin, pull up the testicles or squeeze the vagina, tighten the neck, sink the sternum, and push from the sternum to tilt C7 back.

15. Tuck the chin in to lock the neck, keeping the chest relaxed. With this action the energy moves from the sacrum to C7. Pack the chi at C7 by circling the energy 9 times clockwise and 9 times counterclockwise. This will activate the cranial pump located at the base of the skull (the Jade Pillow, C1), which works in tandem with the sacral pump to move cerebrospinal fluid up and down the spine and around the brain.

16. With your neck still locked, inhale, packing energy up to your Jade Pillow. Collect the energy here, circling 9 times clockwise and 9 times counterclockwise at C1.

17. Inhale 10 percent and pull the energy up to the crown of the head. Turn both eyes upward and look inward, to the area of the pineal gland. Collect the energy here, circling it 9 times clockwise and 9 times counterclockwise, until you are out of breath.

18. Now exhale slowly. Relax the neck, the anus, the groin, and the urogenital diaphragm. Keep the tongue at the palate.

19. Regulate the breath by practicing abdominal breathing, but this time inhale less and exhale more. Concentrate your attention at the third eye. Guide the energy from the tongue past the throat and the heart center and down to the solar plexus. Collect the chi in the solar plexus, circling 9 times clockwise and 9 times counterclockwise.

20. With the toes spread, open the knees slightly so that you can feel the force in the ankle joints. This will enable you to grasp the ground with the feet and feel the soles press down to the ground. Force the energy to flow downward; put dynamic tension on the small and big balls of the feet and the outer edges of the feet. Make sure you do not lift any of the feet's nine points of contact off the ground.

21. Maintaining this position, stand still as you feel the energy travel out of the ground up the legs and into the spinal cord, through C7 at the base of the neck out into the arms, up to the pineal and pituitary glands, and then down the front of the body to the navel. Feel heat in the navel. Continue circulating the energy for as long as you wish.

22. Practice Bone Breathing.

23. Practice the Power Exercise.

24. Stand erect, keeping the tongue at the palate, and collect energy in the navel. Women place the left palm at the navel and the right palm over the left. Men place the right palm over the navel and the left palm over that.

25. Begin to walk slowly around the room, breathing normally. Stroke the chest downward with the palms of the hands to prevent any congestion from developing there. Walking about the room will distribute the chi and give the stressed muscles a chance to recuperate (fig. 3.58). Keep the muscles in a state of soft tension, remembering that this kind of softness breeds strength.

In time you should be able to do Embracing the Tree in two breaths: one down the front of the body and one up the back. With practice you can do the whole process in just one breath.

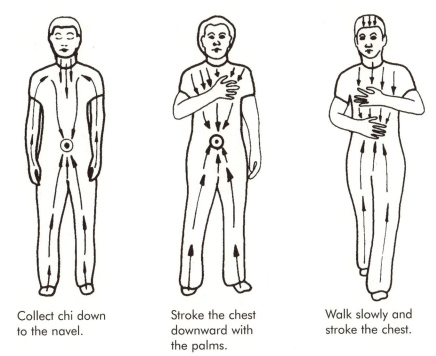

Collect chi down to the navel.

Stroke the chest downward with the palms.

Walk slowly and stroke the chest.

Fig. 3.58. Collecting and distributing the chi

Summary: Embracing the Tree with Chi Condensing and Circulating

1. Stand with the feet shoulder-width apart. Bend the knees, pressing the sacrum down.
2. Position the arms as if they are encircling a tree; hold the thumbs up and relax the fingers, barely permitting them to touch. Relax the chest and hold the head erect.
3. Place the tongue on the palate. Practice abdominal breathing 9 or 18 times. Feel the sexual organs move up and down with the breath.
4. Inhale 10 percent to your navel, keeping the abdomen flat and pressing the diaphragm downward as you pull the sex organs up. Inhale and pull up the left and right sides of the anus. Pack and

wrap the chi at the kidneys, then collect energy at the navel.

5. Breathe into the lower abdomen, without spiraling. Breathe into the perineum and feel it bulge out.

6. Exhale through the back of the legs and the feet. Feel the palms and soles breathing.

7. Suck energy from the Earth through K1, Bubbling Springs. "Claw" the ground with the toes as you inhale and circle the energy 9 times clockwise and 9 times counterclockwise at Bubbling Springs (Kidney 1). The spirals on the soles of the feet move in the same direction.

8. Inhale, bringing energy to the knees. Lock the knees; do not spiral at the knees.

9. Inhale up to the perineum; circle the energy there 9 times clockwise and 9 times counterclockwise. Feel the bulge at the perineum.

10. Exhale. Harmonize the breath and be aware of the soles and palms breathing.

11. Inhale and pull up the left and right sides of the anus, packing the back and kidneys.

12. Inhale up to the sacrum. Tilt the sacrum back, packing it. Circle the energy 9 times clockwise and 9 times counterclockwise. This will strengthen and activate the sacral pump.

13. Inhale to T11, inflating the kidney area. Press outward at T11, then spiral 9 times clockwise and 9 times counterclockwise.

14. Inhale to C7, pushing from the sternum to tilt C7 back, straightening the curve at the neck.

15. Lock the neck by tucking the chin. Circle the chi 9 times clockwise and 9 times counterclockwise.

16. Inhale to the Jade Pillow (C1), clench the teeth tight, and squeeze the skull and the temple bones to strengthen and activate the cranial pump. Circle the energy here 9 times clockwise and 9 times counterclockwise.

17. Inhale to the crown (pineal gland) and circle 9 times clockwise

and 9 times counterclockwise. If you cannot go all the way up on one breath you can pass over the Jade Pillow, or you can take an extra breath where needed until your capacity increases.

18. Exhale with the tongue up to the palate.

19. Regulate the breath. Concentrate on the third eye until you feel the chi energy build up there. Bring the energy down to the solar plexus and circle 9 times clockwise and 9 times counterclockwise. Bring the chi down to the navel. Stand still and maintain this position.

20. Press the soles to the ground. Discipline your mind to move the energy downward.

21. Feel energy flowing up from the ground. Circulate the energy for as long as you wish.

22. Practice Bone Breathing.

23. Practice the Power Exercise.

24. Stand up and bring the energy into the navel, putting your hands over the navel and bringing the feet together. Relax. Collect the energy in the navel area.

25. When you feel calm, walk around and brush the energy downward.

The Importance of Rooting

Rooting is a fundamental practice in the Universal Tao system. Taoist practitioners focus on rootedness. A strong root can be compared to the foundation of a building. The strength of the foundation in part determines how high the building can be built and how difficult it will be to topple.

The principle of rooting is to become like a rod positioned at a 45-degree angle. When you push the end of the rod at a right angle, the force travels into the ground. If your body alignment is joined with the Earth, when the force comes at you it will go right through you and into the ground. The rod is not what is powerful. It is the Earth underneath it that has the power, although naturally the rod has to be strong to pass the force (fig. 4.1).

The foot, the leg, and the knee can all be adjusted to be like a rod angled at 45 degrees, protruding from the ground. No matter what position you are in, always bear in mind that your body must be aligned with the Earth so that the force will not stay in the joints but can pass through the bones to the ground (fig. 4.2). If your body is not aligned so that the force can pass through the structure, you will fall (fig. 4.3).

The more that practitioners can root to Mother Earth, the more balanced their energies will be. Such balance increases healing energy.

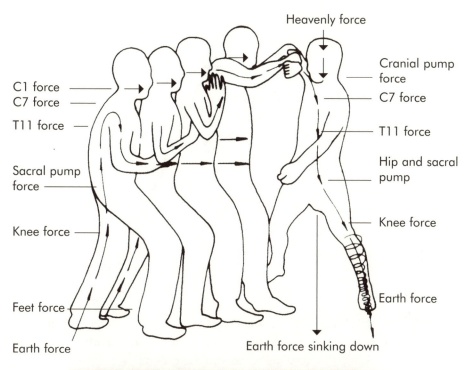

Heavenly force

Cranial pump force

C1 force

C7 force

C7 force

T11 force

T11 force

Hip and sacral pump

Sacral pump force

Knee force

Knee force

Feet force

Earth force

Earth force

Earth force sinking down

Fig. 4.1. With rooting, outside forces are transferred down to the ground through the bone structure.

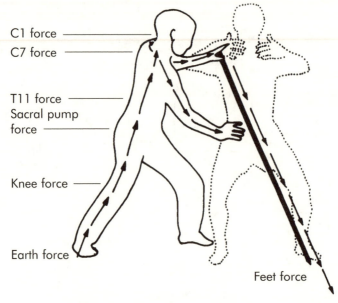

C1 force
C7 force

T11 force
Sacral pump
force

Knee force

Earth force

Feet force

Fig. 4.2. When the leg, knee, and foot are properly aligned at a 45-degree angle to the ground, it is as if your partner is pushing a rod into the ground.

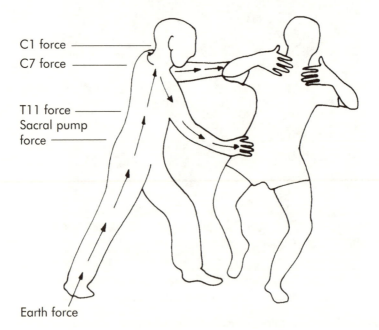

C1 force
C7 force

T11 force
Sacral pump
force

Earth force

Fig. 4.3. If the body is not aligned the force cannot pass through the structure.

After mastering the Rooting Practice, as you move about in your daily life you will feel that you are more in touch with the Earth. You will feel more stable and practical minded. After practicing Iron Shirt Rooting for a while, many Universal Tao students find that they have good balance and that their performance of various physical activities is greatly improved.

In advanced studies, rooting is required for performing the Thrusting Channels and Belt Channels practices, Tai Chi, Buddha Palm, and the higher spiritual practices that draw upon Earth energy, as well as heavenly energy, to transform life force into spiritual energy in order to give birth to the soul and spirit. It is Earth energy that helps the soul and spirit grow. Astral traveling requires rooting; this earthly rootedness serves the soul and spirit the way a control tower serves a space rocket. Those who try to bring chi energy up to the head or to receive heavenly energy without grounding in the Earth become spacey instead of "in tune" with their experience.

Rooting Practice requires two people: one pushes while the other works on his or her stance. Many people will find that one side of the body is weaker than the other, or that the upper part of the body is weaker than the lower body. Always balance your energies by using both sides of the body during practice. Practice on the strong side first so that you will have a reference for improving your weaker side. Gradually you will grow stronger and it will require less effort to maintain your structured position because you will have developed additional muscle fibers and strengthened the tendons, tendon attachment sites, and fascia as one interlinking structure.

When you "root" properly it feels as though you are sucking the ground or have grown a deep tap into the Earth. This is because the whole structure, as a unit, is pressing into the ground. You can feel the entire bone structure sink down to the ground.

With practice you will be able to bring energy along the prescribed course quickly and easily.

PRINCIPLES OF IRON SHIRT ROOTING

The purpose of the Iron Shirt Rooting Practice is to align the bone structure with the joints in order to feel the whole body as one unit.

Stand in the Iron Shirt Horse Stance. When you practice rooting you can stand with the feet slightly wider than the standard position. However, if the feet are too far apart you have to use muscle strength to hold the body together; then, when a force is received, the muscle will hold the force and knock the bones and joints out of alignment. If, on the other hand, the position of the feet is too narrow, you will be using the force of the tendons to help hold the structure together, negatively affecting alignment as well.

When your partner pushes you with force your neck must be relaxed so that the force will not go into the neck, causing pain there. Your bone structure, organs, muscles, tendons, and fascia must work as a whole to hold the position. This will gradually increase your inner strength.

Packing chi into the organs is very important in the practice of rooting. It is particularly important to pack chi into the kidneys and to join the kidneys and K1 (Bubbling Springs) into one line. The navel and the two kidneys must be joined together energetically so that they feel like a large belt fastened across your waist (fig. 4.4). Using chi energy to join the navel, the sides of the waist, the two kidneys, and T11 is basic to rooting. This line of energy is called the chi belt. Without the chi belt the major connection between the upper and lower parts of the body will be lost.

 ## Developing the Chi Belt

To develop the chi belt, pack chi into the left kidney, expand out to the left waist, and then expand toward the front to the navel. Then pack and wrap the right kidney; expand out to the right waist and forward to the navel.

The left and right sides are now energetically connected at the

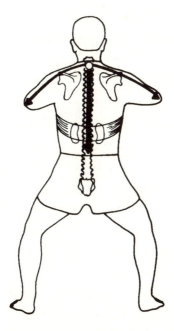

Fig. 4.4. The chi belt joins the whole structure.

navel. As the chi belt expands it connects to T11 and the Door of Life. The navel now feels like a fully inflated tire encased within a big belt.

Mastering the chi belt will help you to stay relaxed in your practice. Once you experience a chi belt in Rooting Practice you will be able to attain rootedness quickly and will not need to use your muscles to join your structure together.

 ## Rooting Stance

1. Assume the Embracing the Tree stance. Sink chi energy down to the lower navel area.
2. Bend the knees and sink down into your lower body. Open the groin by slightly separating the knees.
3. Turn the toes slightly inward. Sink into the knees; feel the connection between the knees and the ankle joints and the connection

down to the feet, to the Kidney 1 point, connecting the kidneys to Bubbling Springs. Feel the weight of your whole body drop down to the ground. The force passes through the bone structure. Feel the bones as sponges that absorb force and direct it into the Earth.

4. In Embracing the Tree posture the hands are held at shoulder level; for Rooting Practice let the elbows sink. Feel the force of the sinking elbows press into the bone structure. If you hold the elbows up you will disconnect from your tendon power.

5. To connect the shoulder joints with the spine, you need to round the scapulae and sink the chest so that the force can be transferred from the shoulders to the scapulae. Connect through the hip joints down to the knee and ankle joints.

6. Line up the shoulder joints by pushing the thumbs out and the pinky fingers in, feeling the pull at the tendons. The wrist joints are connected to the shoulders. Relax the neck, especially the trapezius muscle, so that the force of the connection does not go up to the head. If the neck or head are held tight you will feel as though you were hit by a two-by-four when your partner pushes you, and the force will knock you over. When you relax the neck and join the shoulders with the spine, the force travels down the spine and down into the ground.

7. Extend the neck long and push outward at T11. Keep the sacrum straight without moving the hips. Feel the spine as a flexed bow full of strength.

8. When the groin area is open the hip joints will join with the knees and the feet, and all the joints will join with the Earth. Feel the chi belt encircling the waist and joining the entire structure together.

9. Once you have packed the chi energy to develop a chi belt and aligned the structure as described, have your partner push (not hit) a fist against your sacrum, then against T11, then C7, and finally against the base of the skull to develop awareness of these important centers and their interrelationships. It is important that the sacrum, T11, C7, and the base of the skull become strengthened

and linked together into one line, in order to transfer an oncoming force (or your partner's force) to the ground.

When your partner pushes you, do not lean toward him. Trust your structure and feel your entire body knit itself into one unit. Feel the bones like sponges absorbing the force and passing the force along the bone structure to the ground. When you feel that force, open the knee a little and feel the knees connected to the earth. Feel the energy pass to the ground.

When a person pushes you a force is passed to you. The tendency as your partner pushes you is to counter his or her force by pushing the elbows out; however, this action moves you out of alignment. When you feel your partner's energy come at you, keep the elbows down and redirect the force back to the scapulae and to the spine. Your partner's force, then, will not push you out of alignment.

BUILDING ROOTEDNESS

Being the hub of the nervous system, the spinal cord is the agent that joins together all of the various parts of the body. The spine consists of the vertebrae, small bones that are held together by muscles, tendons, and fascia.

Most of the Universal Tao exercises are not meant solely for strengthening the spine. But Iron Shirt Chi Kung is designed to strengthen the entire bone structure, and especially the spine. Many people have weak spines, which causes bad posture and breathing problems and exacerbates weakness in the organs. In actual fact, weak organs are the original cause of a weak spine. Poor posture becomes a vicious cycle: organs are kept in a weakened state because chi cannot circulate to and through the various body systems.

Iron Shirt practices protect the organs, which generate vital chi; they recharge the organs through packing chi into them; they circulate chi up the spine, strengthening the nervous system; and they create storage space for the chi energy by burning fat. The following exercises strengthen the most important spinal centers: the sacrum, T11, C7, and C1.

 ## Strengthening the Sacral Pump

The sacrum is the very important pump that moves chi into the spine.

1. To begin this exercise, assume the Embracing the Tree stance.
2. Bring the sacrum into your awareness. Pack the kidneys with chi to develop a chi belt.
3. Now have your partner put a fist directly on the sacrum. Without moving your hips, slowly push your sacrum toward the back, pushing against your partner's hand (fig. 4.5). Your partner should gradually increase the force until you grow more powerful in the sacrum area, increasing to the maximum you can withstand without pushing you over. Hold this position for 1 to 2 minutes, breathing normally.

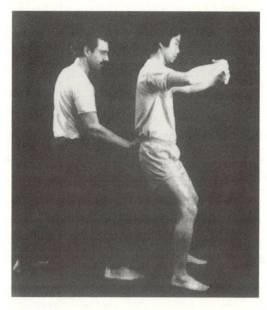

Fig. 4.5. Push your sacrum toward the back, pushing against your partner's hand.

4. The sacral pump transfers your partner's force through your bone structure to the ground. Be aware of the force transferring from your sacrum to your legs, your feet, and your toes. Exert force from your toes back up the feet to your heels, to your legs, and to your sacrum.

5. When your partner releases the force against the sacrum, feel that the sacrum is open and feel how the chi flows up the spine. Rest for a while, maintaining awareness of these sensations.

At the advanced levels of this practice you can be very relaxed— you will have no need to pack chi before beginning the practice. You will simply feel the force from your partner pass from the sacrum to the ground and feel the energy come up from the ground to resist that force. Your bones actively channel that energy upward from the Earth (fig. 4.6). Feel yourself resisting your partner's force through your bones. Do not lean toward your partner.

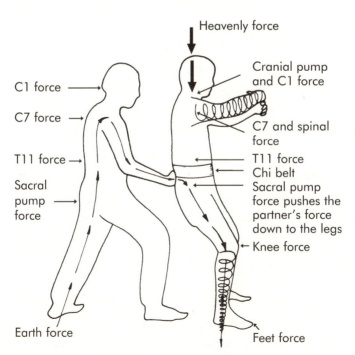

Fig. 4.6. The play of forces in strengthening the sacral pump

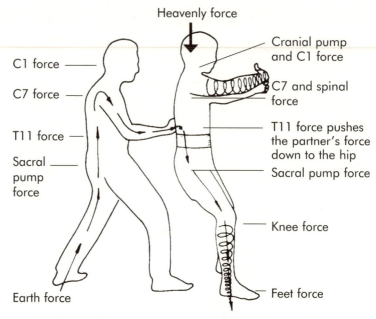

Heavenly force

C1 force

C7 force

T11 force

Sacral pump force

Earth force

Cranial pump and C1 force

C7 and spinal force

T11 force pushes the partner's force down to the hip

Sacral pump force

Knee force

Feet force

Fig. 4.7. The force of T11 transfers your partner's force to the ground.

 ## Strengthening T11

The eleventh thoracic vertebra, T11, is regarded by the Taoists as a pump that aids in moving energy to the upper body.

Assume the position for Embracing the Tree and pack the kidneys with chi to develop a chi belt. Now have your partner push his fist against T11 as you press back with that area of the spine. Your partner's force is transferred to the ground through the bone structure by the force of T11. This work is done by the spine, not by the whole body (fig. 4.7). Do not lean toward your partner.

 ## Strengthening C7

The seventh cervical vertebra is considered the point at which all the tendons of the body join together. By strengthening this part of the body, the tendons, the fascia, and the neck will be strengthened. The seventh cervical vertebra is also the energetic point of connection between the arms/hands and the spinal cord.

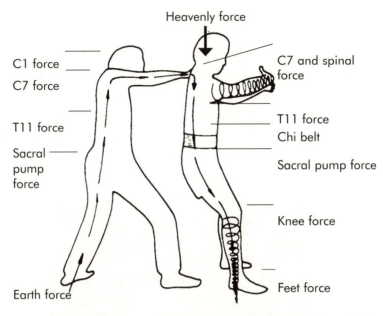

Heavenly force

C1 force

C7 force

C7 and spinal force

T11 force

T11 force
Chi belt

Sacral pump force

Sacral pump force

Knee force

Earth force

Feet force

Fig. 4.8. Your partner's force is transferred down to the ground through the bone structure by the force of C7.

Assume the position for Embracing the Tree and pack with chi pressure as described. Your partner then uses a palm (not the fist) to push against C7 as you press back into the palm from this same point. The force of C7 transfers your partner's force to the ground.

Hold this position for as long as you can (fig. 4.8). Communicate with your partner when you are ready to release.

 ## Strengthening the Cranial Pump

The cranial pump has long been regarded by Taoists as a major pump for circulating energy through the body. Minute movements occur at the joints of the cranial bones during breathing. Cranial movement stimulates the production of the cerebrospinal fluid, the fluid that surrounds and nourishes the brain and spinal cord. The cerebrospinal fluid normalizes nerve and energy patterns throughout the body. Strengthening the cranial pump can increase energy and alleviate symptoms such as headaches, sinus problems, visual disturbances, and neck problems.

Assume the position for Embracing the Tree and pack with chi pressure to create a chi ball. Clench the teeth, tighten the neck, and contract the cranium by squeezing the muscles around the skull and pressing the tongue tightly to the roof of the mouth. Have your partner use a palm (not the fist) to push against the base of the skull as you press back into the palm from this same point (fig. 4.9). The force of C1 transfers your partner's force through the bone structure and to the ground.

Fig. 4.9. Your partner's force is transferred down to the ground through the bone structure by the force of C1.

 Left and Right Side Rooting Practice

Assume the stance for Embracing the Tree and pack the kidneys with chi energy to create a chi belt. Your partner stands to one side of you, placing one hand on your shoulder and the other on your hip. Your partner begins by pushing you lightly, then gradually increases to full force. If you are well rooted the force of your partner's push will flow right through your bone structure, down your feet, and into the Earth (fig. 4.10).

If you have learned to direct and absorb energy through the bone structure and into the soles of the feet, you will be able to receive the powerful healing energy created by the blending of your energy, your partner's energy, and Earth energy. Your practice will have acquainted you with feeling the flow of energy as it travels down through the feet into the Earth and then back out of the Earth, up through the feet, and into you.

Have your partner push on the left side first. Practice abdominal breathing and then resume the Embracing the Tree stance. Now your partner pushes you on the right side.

In the beginning you will feel tight and tense. You will need to use Packing Process Breathing, holding the breath to hold your structure together. As your practice improves and you are able to control and direct the energy to the place where your partner is pushing, it will

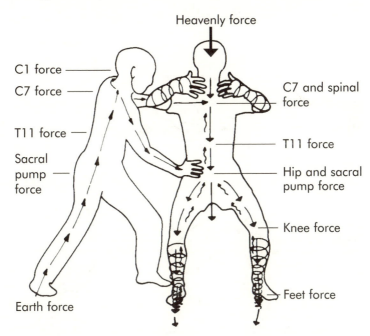

Fig. 4.10. Right side rooting practice

not be necessary to hold the breath, since you will be able to maintain your structure and your rooting without packing and without tensing the muscles at all. If the shoulders and spine are not joined together you will fall.

 ## Front Rooting

Front Rooting primarily trains the front structure to connect more solidly to the Earth. The practice focuses especially on the hands, the ribs, the front of the legs, the soles of the feet, and the toes. Many people find it hard to root to the Earth. To be successful you must feel your partner's force pass to your shoulder, scapulae, spine, sacrum, hips, and legs as one line.

Assume the Embracing the Tree stance; pack the kidneys with chi energy to create a chi belt. Have your partner push you on both wrists using both palms (fig. 4.11). Use the force of C7 and the spine to push the partner's force down to the hip.

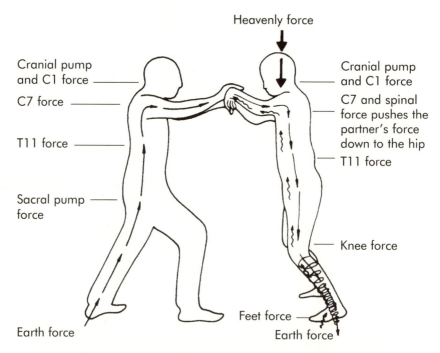

Fig. 4.11. Transferring the force to the ground in Front Rooting

Front Rooting is difficult and can take a lot of practice to master. In the beginning your partner should apply only a minor force, increasing gradually as your skill develops. Gradual force will open the leg channels and hand channels and join them together. The spinal cord and C7 play a very important role in the Front Rooting practice.

 ## One-Legged Rooting

Stand on one leg and raise the opposite arm, making a circle with the arm as in Embracing the Tree stance. Sink the chest. Feel both arms and both legs connected. Sink down into the Earth. When your partner pushes you, guide that force down to the ground (fig. 4.12).

In this practice the arm, the scapula, the spine, and the leg join together in one line, similar to a rod sticking into the ground (fig. 4.13). When you push the rod the force transfers to the ground. If the fascia and tendons are not strong, the structure will bend or break when pushed. When you are proficient at aligning all of the joints,

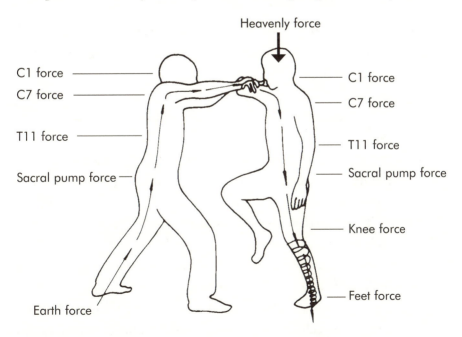

Fig. 4.12. Transferring the force to the ground in One-Legged Rooting

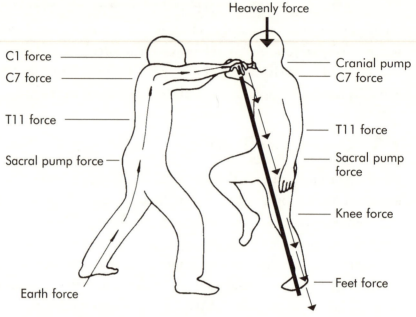

Heavenly force

C1 force

C7 force

T11 force

Sacral pump force

Earth force

Cranial pump

C7 force

T11 force

Sacral pump force

Knee force

Feet force

Fig. 4.13. The arm, the scapula, the spine, and the leg align to transfer the force to the ground.

no matter where the force directed at you comes from, you will be able to redirect it down to the Earth rather than letting it break your alignment.

COLLECTING CHI ENERGY AFTER PRACTICE

After each practice be sure to stand erect and silent for a few moments. Concentrate your attention on the navel, collecting the chi there. As the chi sinks down, use your palms to stroke your chest from top to bottom. This prevents congestion at the chest and heart as well as other side effects, such as heartburn, headache, and eye pain. Move your hands to release the congestion and walk around until you feel the energy settle down.

After practicing Iron Shirt, take time to do the Microcosmic Orbit meditation, also called the Awaken Healing Energy meditation, as described in chapter 2. During Iron Shirt Practice you generate tremendous energy, which flows upward and can become trapped in the brain and the chest, especially in the heart. With practice you will be able to direct the energy down to the navel from all sides and collect it there. As your practice of Iron Shirt progresses you will continue to open the navel area for storing energy to be utilized in the higher spiritual practices.

Sitting and Standing Positions for Collecting Energy

When you have finished the Iron Shirt Practice, you should sit down to collect the energy that you have built up (fig. 4.14).

Sit on the edge of a chair, using your sitting bones to find that delicate point of balance that will help hold you erect. Men should sit far enough forward to allow the scrotum to hang freely. Women should also sit forward and should keep the genitalia covered to avoid energy loss. The back must be comfortably erect, the head bowed slightly forward. Rest your hands in your lap.

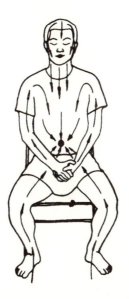

Fig. 4.14. Collect the energy at the navel.

You might also choose to stand as you collect energy. If you do, stand straight and place the palm on the navel. Women place the left palm on the navel; men place the right palm on the navel. Smile down to the organs and bring the energy to them. In both positions, touch the tongue to the palate.

Starting at the navel, let the energy circulate down to the perineum and up the sacrum to the spine, to the top of the crown, down the third eye to the tongue, to the heart, to the solar plexus, and finally back to the navel. Circulate the chi this way several times, then collect the chi at the navel by circulating it 36 times outward and 24 times inward to the navel. Men should spiral the energy out in a clockwise direction, making 36 revolutions, then spiral inward in the opposite direction 24 times, ending and collecting the energy at the navel.

Women should make the same action, but begin by spiraling the energy out from the navel in a counterclockwise direction and spiraling back to the navel in a clockwise direction.

The Iron Shirt Chi Kung Postures

Now that we have learned the fundamental stances for alignment and wrapping and packing chi, we are ready to learn a series of postures specifically for building chi in the body. These postures have been distilled from a group of forty-nine exercises that were passed down from teacher to student in the Taoist tradition for thousands of years. Practicing these postures diligently and with care to the specifics of skeletal and tendon alignment and breathwork will help you make great strides in building the foundation of your physical body.

Some of these postures have a yang and a yin component. The yang position is a dynamic, active position; the yin component provides a balancing stretch and time for harmonizing the breath.

Many of the adjunct rooting exercises described in this chapter require a partner to be practiced most effectively. It is always good to choose a partner who is generally your equal in size and strength.

Be sure to collect the energy as instructed at the end of every exercise.

HOLDING THE GOLDEN URN

The yang aspect of Holding the Golden Urn joins the pinky fingers to a line that runs up to and around the ears and then down the sides of

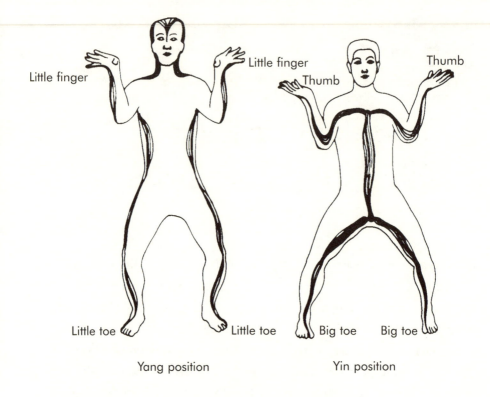

Little finger

Little finger

Thumb

Thumb

Little toe

Little toe

Big toe

Big toe

Yang position

Yin position

Fig. 5.1. Holding the Golden Urn

the body to the small toes. The yin posture strengthens the thumb line by joining it to the chest, the navel, and the big toes (fig. 5.1). These lines are very important in holding the tendinomuscular and skeletal structures together. When connected, these two lines issue force on the sides and the front of the body.

In practicing Holding the Golden Urn we use one breath but many inhalations. This means that you continue inhaling until you can take in no more oxygen, then you exhale. This is regarded as one breath.

Throughout the exercise your tongue should be touching your palate to keep the energy flowing. Follow your practice of the yang position with the yin position.

Holding the Golden Urn: Yang Position

1. Assume a Horse Stance with your feet positioned shoulder-width apart. The toes point inward and the knees separate and are locked, as described in Embracing the Tree.
2. Rotate your shoulders to bring your elbows forward. Your forearms are held at approximately 30 degrees from your sides. Feel as though you are pressing up strongly through the shoulders without actually moving the arms. The chest sinks down slightly in response to the shoulders rounding forward (fig. 5.2).
3. Lift the forearms and spread the fingers, palms down. Pull the tendons of your little fingers so that the backs of your hands make a flat surface upon which you could support a large golden urn (fig. 5.3). Spreading the fingers and feeling the outward pull through the pinky fingers produces a bracing action that enables you to

Fig. 5.2. Holding the Golden Urn starting position

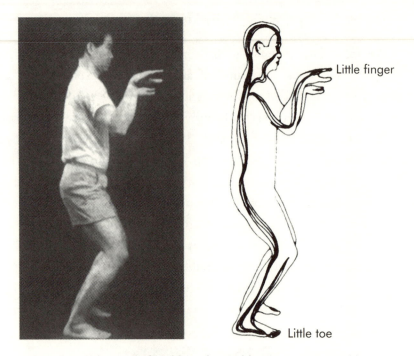

Little finger

Little toe

Fig. 5.3. Side view of Holding the Golden Urn, yang position

sustain considerable weight. The tendon lines that are engaged in this posture connect the small toes and small fingers, bringing more force and energy into them, tightening and strengthening the outer structure. The little fingers may seem weak but, when consciously attended to, they give power to the whole structure.

4. Begin with 9 or 18 rounds of abdominal breathing (fig. 5.4).
5. Exhale and flatten the abdomen. Inhale and, keeping the abdomen flat, pull up the left and right sides of the anus. Bring the chi to pack into and wrap around the kidneys.
6. Inhale and pack the chi into the lower abdominal area, contracting the anus and pulling up on the urogenital diaphragm. Feel energy draw upward from the soles of the feet to the sacrum.
7. Inhale, packing to the sexual organs. Tilt the sacrum back, creating a suction force that pulls energy in and activates the sacral pump. Pull the back part of the anus toward the sacrum.

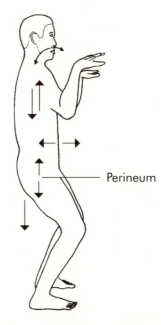

Fig. 5.4. Holding the Golden Urn with abdominal breathing

8. Inhale and pack the chi at the sacrum. Tilt the sacrum back a little bit more.

9. Inhale and pack up to T11, pushing T11 to the back until you feel your spine arched like a flexed bow. (You can use a wall as your guide, pushing T11 to the wall.) Inflate the back with chi pressure, contract the anus, and pull the urogenital diaphragm up. Feel the energy rise from the Bubbling Springs points on the soles of the feet all the way up to T11. Feel a chi belt stretching from T11 to the Door of Life (L2/L3) and from there to the navel and lower abdomen.

10. Inhale, contracting the anus even more and lifting the genitals, drawing more energy up from the feet and packing it into the kidneys and the liver (fig. 5.5).

11. Tilt C7 to the back until you feel a strong connection between C7, T11, and the sacrum. Feel the full strength of the flexed bow of the spine as the chi inflates the entire neck. Hold for a few seconds.

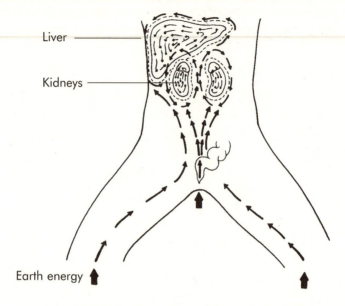

Liver

Kidneys

Earth energy

Fig. 5.5. Draw energy upward through the feet to pack
and wrap at the kidneys and the liver.

12. Inhale and pull up some more, tightening the neck and squeezing
the cranial bones. Clench the teeth and press the tongue to the
roof of the mouth.

13. Inhale. Pull the energy up to the base of the skull and squeeze
more in the cranial bones. Push the neck back. Feel the neck and
base of the skull connected to C7, T11, the sacrum, the knees, and
the feet, feeling them become one flexed bow of strength.

14. Inhale more and tighten, bringing energy up to the crown.

15. Now exhale and relax, then proceed with practice of the yin
position.

Holding the Golden Urn: Yin Position

1. Turn the hands over, palms up, and rotate the hands outward so
that the thumbs now pull back and out to the ears. Stretch the
tendons at the wrists by locking the elbows and the wrists when

turning the hands. The wrists are held as close to a 90-degree angle as possible. The elbows sink and the scapulae are rounded. When you stretch the thumbs you are stretching the tendons of the inner arm. This is the yin position for Holding the Golden Urn (figs. 5.6 and 5.7).

2. Breathe normally. You should feel the energy rush up and over your head, into your arms, and down the front of the body to your navel. Concentrate on the solar plexus. Make sure energy is flowing down from the tongue to the solar plexus and navel along the Microcosmic Orbit.

3. Take 9 inhales and 9 exhales, exhaling more and inhaling less. This is yin breathing. It will help to bring the energy down the front of the body. When the thumb and big toe lines are linked they connect the muscles, tendons, bones, and the spinal cord to operate as a single structure, strengthening the rooting power in the front energy line.

Fig. 5.6. Holding the Golden Urn, yin position

Fig. 5.7. Side view of Holding the Golden Urn, yin position

In the yin position the flow runs from the thumbs to the upper arms, and the big toes connect with the knees, navel, and thumbs. The thumbs connect with the lungs and with tendons that run down the torso and the front of the legs to the big toes.

4. Place your hands over the navel. Collect chi in the navel.
5. Practice Bone Breathing to absorb chi into the bones. Meditate in standing position for a while. If you wish, work on circulating the chi in the Microcosmic Orbit. Then walk around, shaking out the legs and brushing down the chest.

 ## Holding the Golden Urn Rooting Practice

We begin rooting practice with the yang position of Holding the Golden Urn, then move on to the yin position. Using his thumb and index finger, your partner will press against your wrist and your hip. Start with the left side, then challenge the right side.

Yang Position Rooting

Assume the yang position for Holding the Golden Urn and pack energy into the abdomen and the spinal cord and up to the neck. Feel the strength of the spine as a flexed bow.

Now brace your tendon lines by extending your pinky fingers outward strongly. Have your partner attempt to uproot you by gradually applying pressure against the wrist and the hip (fig. 5.8).

Yin Position Rooting

With your body connected with your partner's in Yang Position Rooting, turn your hands over and transfer your partner's force to the ground through your bone structure. Feel the thumbs link with the big toes. Feel the thumb gaining force. Your body's entire front line—starting from the thumb and continuing to the arm, hand, front of the head, ear, armpit, front of the hip, and the leg to the big toe—is

Fig. 5.8. Rooting practice from the side in the yang
position of Holding the Golden Urn

connected and pitted against your partner's force. Have your partner
attempt to push you out of the stance by gradually applying pressure
against the wrist and the hip.

Back and Front Pushing

Back Pushing strengthens the spinal cord, the pinky fingers and small
toes, and the fascia of the back.

Return to the yang position. Press the big and small toes downward and feel that you are exerting force on the small toes and on the
small fingers. Have your partner gradually exert force at your back
while you are in the stance (fig. 5.9). Notice the feeling of support
along the tendon lines. Keeping the stance, have your partner push
your chest to continue developing your rootedness (fig. 5.10).

Exhale and relax. When you are ready, return to the yang position. Quickly pack energy into the entire back and to the neck. Now
move into the yin position by turning the hands over and pulling the
thumbs back. Feel the relationship between the thumbs and the big

Fig. 5.9. Back Pushing in
Holding the Golden Urn, yang
position

Fig. 5.10. Front Pushing
increases the thumb and
tendon power.

toes. Maintain awareness of this relationship as your partner exerts
force on your hands.

Summary of Holding the Golden Urn

Yang Position

1. Stand with feet shoulder-width apart.
2. Rotate the shoulders, bringing your elbows forward.
3. Lift the forearms and spread the fingers, palms down.
4. Stand here and practice 9 or 18 rounds of abdominal breathing.
5. Inhale, flattening the abdomen. Pull up on the anus, bringing chi to pack and wrap at the kidneys.
6. Inhale into the lower abdomen.
7. Inhale, packing to the sexual organs.
8. Inhale, tilt the sacrum, and pack the sacrum.
9. Inhale and pack T11 and the kidney area. Feel a chi belt stretching from T11 to L2/L3 and the navel and lower abdomen.

10. Inhale, packing more energy to the kidneys and liver.
11. Inhale and lock the neck. Bring the energy up to C7 and inflate the neck.
12. Inhale to the Jade Pillow, squeezing the skull and the temple bones.
13. Inhale to the crown.
14. Exhale and relax, then proceed to the yin position.

Yin Position

1. Turn the hands over, with the wrists locked. Stretch the thumbs to bring energy up the inside of the arms to the collarbones, down the sides of the sternum to the navel, and down the insides of the thighs to the lower legs and to the big toes.
2. Take 9 breaths, exhaling more than you inhale.
3. Place your hands over your navel and collect the energy.
4. Practice Bone Breathing
5. Meditate in standing position, then shake out the legs and brush down the chest.

GOLDEN TURTLE AND WATER BUFFALO

These postures energize the fasciae of the legs and back; strengthen the spinal cord, sacrum, kidneys, and adrenal glands; and energize the neck and head and the toes and the tendons of the feet. People with high blood pressure should consult a physician before attempting to practice the Golden Turtle posture.

You may feel excessive strain in the thighs, back, or hip joints when you first begin to practice the Golden Turtle and Water Buffalo positions, even if you are not sinking very deeply into the pose. If this is the case for you, practice with a chair or table in front of you on which you can rest your arms (fig. 5.11). This support will enable you to gradually work into the position without strain.

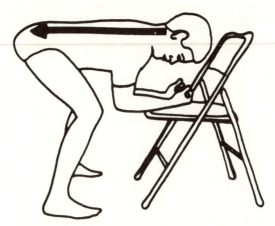

Fig. 5.11. If you feel strain in the thighs, back, or hip joints when practicing
the Golden Turtle and Water Buffalo positions,
rest your arms on a chair or a table.

The Golden Turtle is a posture that many people in the West find
very difficult to do well. The squatting position is intense for those
who don't use the groin and thighs this way much of the time—which
is the majority of us. In Eastern countries people squat when they eat,
when they defecate, as they give birth. It is a much more common-
place daily action, and one that is most beneficial for the body. The
exercises on pages 164 and 165 (fig. 5.13) are warmup exercises for
the Golden Turtle position; they open the body properly for executing this posture. You might find them most helpful to practice before
trying the Golden Turtle posture.

 ## The Golden Turtle Immersing in Water: Yang Position

1. Stand with your feet shoulder-width apart. Position your tongue
   on the roof of your mouth.
2. Begin abdominal breathing, breathing in and out 9 or 18 times,
   inhaling more air than you exhale.
3. On your last exhale, keep the abdomen flattened to the spine. As

you inhale tighten the fists, fold the forearms against the upper arms, round the back, and sink the chest.

4. Now exhale and bend forward as you straighten the back, so that the line from the coccyx to the base of the skull is parallel to the floor (fig. 5.12). Reach forward on that same line from the crown of the head. It is most important that you keep the back straight and parallel to the floor. This may be difficult to feel at first; practice in front of a mirror once in a while to help develop your internal feeling of this spinal alignment.

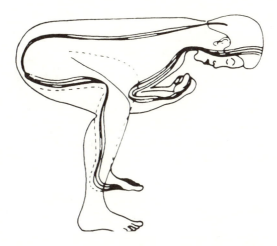

Fig. 5.12. The muscle-tendon meridian activated in the
Golden Turtle position

5. Keep the forearms folded onto the upper arms during the course of this exercise (fig. 5.14). (If you are resting your forearms on a chair or a table, the forearms will not be touching your upper arms.) Keep the armpits open enough to fit a pigeon's egg or other similarly sized object there. Expand the scapulae. The back is energized with chi.

6. Lock the sacrum and open the knees so that you can feel the weight of the body sink down to the hips, to the knees, to the feet, and finally to the ground. The spine should be parallel to the ground.

a. From the basic stance, with the outside edges of the feet parallel, squat down, placing the elbows between the knees with the palms together. Keep the back as parallel to the floor as possible and your eyes looking up. Press out with the elbows resisted by the knees. Press and resist for two seconds, then release and relax.

b. Hook both elbows around the outside of the legs with the forearms behind the knees (front view).

c. Side view

d. Clasp the forearm or elbow with the opposite hand. Bring the head and tail down and toward each other as if looking at your tail. This is very important for protecting your back. Let the shoulder blades be your uppermost point.

e. Pull up strongly, forcing T11 and the mid-back upward against the resistance of the thighs, head, and sacrum. Pull and resist for only two seconds and relax.

Fig. 5.13. This exercise will help in executing the Golden Turtle. For maximum results, practice the sequence shown here, repeating the entire sequence three times.

f. Unlock the arms and bring them to the sides with the forearms rotated so that the palms face the floor. Pull the shoulder blades together.

g. Bring the elbows and head up.

h. Press the elbows up hard, lifting the head and looking forward while pressing the sternum forward. Hold two seconds and relax (side view).

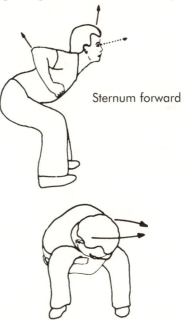

Sternum forward

i. Front view

j. Lock the arms around one knee, clasping the elbows around the knee while looking at the floor.

k. Keep looking at the floor while you pull your ear and tail to the side opposite the knee you are holding, resisting with the knee. After two seconds place the hand on the floor, wag the tail to relax, and then repeat the exercise on the opposite side. Again, wag the tail to relax the spine. During the exercise, the whole spinal column, from the head to the tail, should form a curve like the letter C, parallel to the floor, and you should feel a stretch on the sides of the spine and the neck.

Fig. 5.14. Position of forearms in the Golden Turtle

Pull the energy into the groin area, the sexual center of the body. Tuck the chin and set the neck firmly in position. Press the elbows outward against the inside of the knees while simultaneously pressing the knees inward, equalizing the force. Neither should press harder than the other.

7. Inhale 10 percent and pack the energy in the abdominal region, at the navel. Hold until you are out of breath.

8. Inhale and pack down to the lower abdomen.

9. Inhale, pack at the perineum, and pull on the sexual organs more tightly. Pull Mother Earth energy up to the perineum.

10. Inhale, pack at the sacrum, and tilt the sacrum. Pull up the sex organs more firmly.

11. Inhale and pack at T11, the area of the kidneys and adrenal glands. Press T11 to the back. Feel the entire spine as a fully flexed bow. Inflate the lower back with chi pressure and energize the kidneys.

12. Inhale and pack at C7. Tighten the neck and the cranial bones. Clench your teeth.

13. Inhale and pack to the Jade Pillow, the base of the skull.

14. Inhale up to the crown (fig. 5.15).

15. Now harmonize the breath with abdominal breathing, letting the body relax with the internal flow of chi.

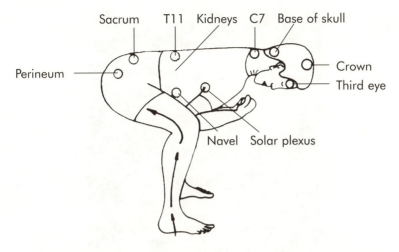

Sacrum   T11   Kidneys   C7   Base of skull

Perineum

Crown

Third eye

Navel   Solar plexus

Fig. 5.15. Energy centers activated during Golden Turtle practice

 ## The Water Buffalo Emerging from the Water: Yin Position

1. Once you have packed the energy to the head in Golden Turtle Immersing in Water, exhale and look slightly upward, releasing the lock in the neck. Extend the arms down in front of you, the backs of the hands facing forward and the fingertips touching the perineum and the anus or touching the ground (fig. 5.16). Keep the groin open. This is the Water Buffalo.

2. Rest the tongue on the palate and relax. Inhale more air than you exhale, breathing directly into the groin area. In this position the groin is quite open, allowing you to breathe down to the lower part of the body, energizing the sexual organs and increasing circulation. Breathe easily and feel the energy descend to the navel and perineum, activating the lower abdomen and strengthening circulation there. The urogenital and pelvic diaphragms, which hold the sexual organs, bladder, and large and small intestines in place, become activated as well.

3. When your breath has harmonized, close your eyes. Slowly extend

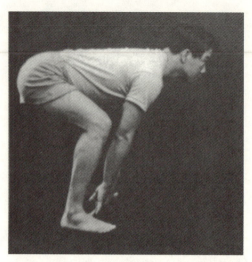

Fig. 5.16. Side view of Water Buffalo

your knees to bring yourself to a standing position. Rise slowly to avoid becoming dizzy.

4. Once you are standing erect, work up some saliva. Then press the neck back as you swallow down to the navel with a guttural sound. Feel the saliva shoot down to the navel and burn with chi power.

5. Place your hands over the navel. Collect chi in the navel.

6. Practice Bone Breathing to absorb chi into the bones. Meditate in standing position for a while. If you wish, work on circulating the chi in the Microcosmic Orbit. Then walk around, shaking out the legs and brushing down the chest.

Rooting Practices

Golden Turtle Rooting

In the Golden Turtle Position the elbows are held tightly pressed against both thighs so that you can feel the energy concentrated in the groin area. The spine is horizontal to the ground (fig. 5.17). Pack chi along the entire back.

Have your partner stand on your left side and place one hand on

Fig. 5.17. Front view of Golden Turtle. Energy is concentrated in the groin and the spine is horizontal to the ground.

your shoulder and the other hand on your hip (fig. 5.18). As your partner begins to exert force, lock your sacrum by drawing it under. Open your knees slightly and adjust your feet to channel your partner's force down to the ground. Become one with the Earth. Ask your partner to increase the pressure to the maximum that you can take without being pushed off balance. Like a sponge, the bone structure absorbs the force and transfers it to the ground. Your partner should continue to exert force until you are ready to rest.

The Turtle Position strengthens the entire back and spine. When your partner pushes from one side—say, from the left—feel the force travel through to the opposite side of the body: from the left shoulder and scapula through the spine to the right scapula, then down the spine to the right hip, thigh, leg, and foot and down to the ground. Feel the sole of the foot breathing and "claw" down with the toes into the ground. If the pressure is too forceful the left foot will uproot. If you feel this happening, push down through the left hip, thigh, and leg to exert more pressure into the earth through the left foot.

Come back into Turtle Position and have your partner exert force gradually on your right side. (When you practice this exercise always balance the body by working both the left and right sides. Remember

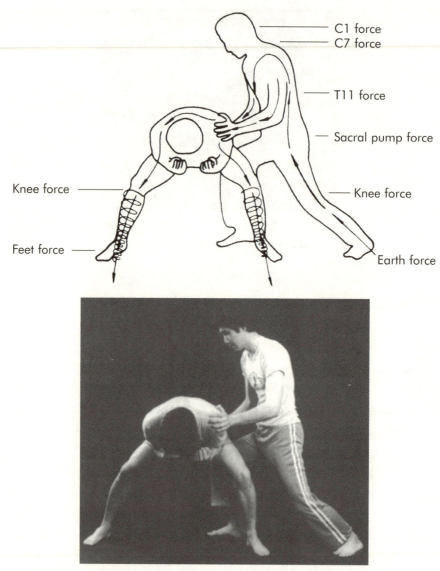

C1 force
C7 force

T11 force

Sacral pump force

Knee force

Knee force

Feet force

Earth force

Fig. 5.18. Golden Turtle rooting practice

that one side is generally stronger than the other.) The purpose of this practice is not for your partner to push you over but to let you feel where the force comes from so that you can direct the force through your body and into the Earth. When force is applied gradually you are able to feel where the force is moving through the body, allowing you to realign or relax that part of the body in order to let the force pass through.

Once you can successfully direct force from any part of your body into the Earth, you will begin to recognize how to reabsorb the force from the Earth. The force that your partner pushes you with, when directed to the Earth, can be reabsorbed back from the Earth and becomes more powerful than before. This energy can be used for self-healing or to counteract a force that comes at you. You can also pass that force to your partner for healing.

Once you become adept in this practice and you feel your body's structure knitted together as one piece, you will feel the muscles relax and find no need for Packing Breathing. If you simply concentrate on the chi flow and relax, the force will pass through the bone structure.

After each round of pushing by your partner, go back to the Water Buffalo position. The chin is lifted, the shoulders relax, and the hands drop down toward the floor. The hands can also touch the sexual organs, which will strengthen the energy of the pelvic and urogenital diaphragms. Breathe deeply to the groin area to strengthen the sexual/creative energy.

⊙ Golden Turtle Front Rooting

In order to strengthen the frontal aspect of this posture, have your partner place one hand on each shoulder and gradually exert force (fig. 5.19). To maintain this difficult position you must feel the connection of the shoulders to the scapulae and of the spine to the sacrum and the hips. Front rooting is more difficult than side rooting and requires more practice. The feet are very important in front rooting; with practice you can maintain the feet's firm contact with the ground.

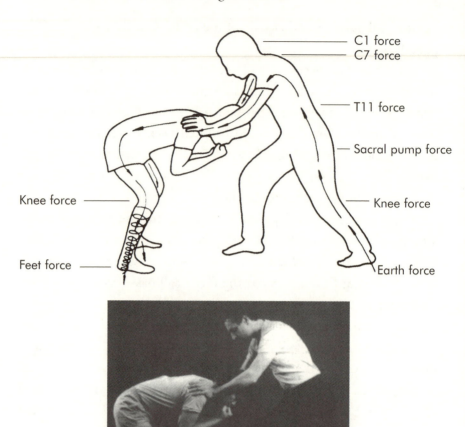

C1 force
C7 force

T11 force

Sacral pump force

Knee force

Knee force

Feet force

Earth force

Fig. 5.19. Golden Turtle front rooting

Summary: Golden Turtle and Water Buffalo

Golden Turtle Immersing in Water: Yang Position

1. Place the tongue on the roof of the mouth.
2. In a standing position, practice lower abdominal breathing for 9 or 18 rounds, inhaling more air than you exhale.
3. Flatten the abdomen to the spine as you exhale. Inhale, abdo-

men to spine, as you clench the fists, bend the arms in close to the body, round the back, and sink the chest.

4. Exhale and bend forward with a straight back.
5. Inhale and pack to the navel.
6. Inhale and pack to the lower abdomen.
7. Inhale and pack to the perineum.
8. Inhale and pack to the sacrum. Tilt the sacrum to activate the sacral pump.
9. Inhale and pack to T11.
10. Inhale and pack to C7.
11. Inhale and pack to the Jade Pillow.
12. Inhale and pack to the crown of the head.
13. Inhale and pack more along the back.
14. Harmonize the breath with abdominal breathing, then practice Water Buffalo.

Water Buffalo Emerging from the Water: Yin Position

1. Exhale and look slightly upward.
2. Keeping the back straight, reach the arms down, the back of the hands facing forward. You can also touch the groin area while maintaining the same back position.
3. Practice lower abdominal breathing while focusing on the groin area.
4. Close your eyes and stand up slowly. Put the hands on the navel area and collect the energy.
5. Practice Bone Breathing.
6. Practice the Power Exercise.
7. Meditate in standing position, then shake out the legs and brush down the chest.

GOLDEN PHOENIX WASHES ITS FEATHERS

The Golden Phoenix position strengthens both sides of the ribs, from the armpits down to the sides of the hips, and packs chi pressure into all of the major organs. On the left side you pack, wrap, and squeeze chi into the left kidney, the spleen, the left lung, and the heart; on the right side you are strengthening the right kidney, the liver, and the right lung.

Golden Phoenix Washes Its Feathers also exercises the fingers, toes, tendons, and the tongue (which is one of the major muscles of the body). While the pinky fingers may be small, they can activate many tendons, especially along the sides of the body.

Golden Phoenix Practice: Yang Position

1. Assume the Iron Shirt Horse Stance (fig. 5.20a). Place your arms at your sides. Practice abdominal breathing to fan the energy.

2. Place your arms in front of your body with the backs of the hands facing one another. Sweep the arms out to both sides, pulling up through the perineum and anus. Turn the hands over so that the wrists are straight (fig. 5.20b).

3. Now turn the palms to face upward and in toward the body, as though you were gathering something up under the armpits. The pinky fingers point up toward the ceiling (fig. 5.20c). Feel the pull of the tendons all the way up the arms to the ears, around the ears, and down the sides of the body to the small toes. The scapulae are rounded. The neck muscles and the trapezius muscles are relaxed so that the hands and the arms are connected. The elbows are bent out to the side.

4. Inhale while you pull up the left and right sides of the anus and bring the sexual energy from the testicles or ovaries to the kidneys. Pack this energy into the kidneys and to the adrenals, which are located at the top of the kidneys on about the same level as the solar plexus. Bring the palms up along the sides of the body, feeling the pull of the tendons on the insides of the arms up to the elbows, the pinky fingers, and the thumbs.

5. Inhale higher toward the armpits (fig. 5.20d), pulling the sexual energy from the testicles or ovaries to the kidneys and up to the

a. Assume the Iron Shirt Horse Stance.

b. Sweep the arms out to both sides.

c. Turn palms face up and in toward the body, with the pinky fingers pointing up.

d. Bring hands as close to the armpits as you can; palms continue to face up.

Fig. 5.20. The Golden Phoenix exercise

e. Rotate the hands medially; the palms face outward.

f. Push from the sternum to C7, extending the arms.

g. Side view of fully extended arms

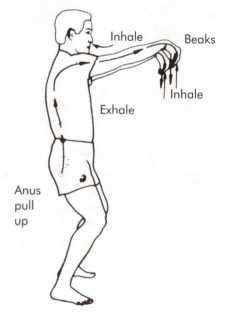

h. Gather the fingers and form "beaks."

i. Front view of pulling the beaks

j. Pull the beaks closer to your body.

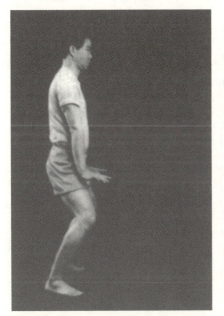

k. Exhale as you release the beaks. Press your arms against the front of your body.

l. Front view of the arms pressed down

spleen on the left side and the liver on the right. Pack the chi into the organs and then wrap the chi around them. The palms still face up and the tendons of the pinky fingers stretch toward the ceiling. Inhale as you bring the hands as close to the armpits as possible, pulling the sexual energy up to the heart and to the lungs. Fill the lungs with chi. Feel the entire rib cage and the armpits bulge up as they fill with chi.

6. When you get as close to the armpits as you can, exhale while maintaining the contraction in the anus and the pull on the genitals. Rotate the hands medially. Face the palms outward (fig. 5.20e, page 176), pulling from the scapulae, which are connected to the Earth. The forearms are straight; the elbows are back; the wrists are locked; the knees are open.

7. Push from the sternum to C7, feeling the force come from the ground up into the heels, the sacrum, the spinal cord, the scapulae, and the hands (fig. 5.20f). As you push, extend your arms and exhale using the first healing sound, the lung sound: "Sssssss." (A complete explanation of the six healing sounds is provided in the book *Taoist Ways to Transform Stress into Vitality*.) At this point you should feel your body to be like one interlocking unit, from the palms to the heels. This is the meaning of the word *structure*.

8. When the arms are fully extended (figs. 5.20g), inhale as you contract the middle of the anus and pull the sexual organs upward. Feel the pull at the tips of the fingers of both hands.

9. Now gather the fingers to the thumbs and press them together into a small point, exerting more force on the pinky fingers and the tips of all the fingers (figs. 5.20h and 5.20i). (We refer to this finger position as a beak.) Feel the pulling force in the anus and in the tips of the fingers combine into a single force.

10. Inhale as you pull the beaks inward from the elbows and contract the middle part of the anus. Feel the force of the anus and the sexual organ pull the beaks in.

11. Inhale again, pull your beaks closer to the body, further tightening the anus and genital areas. While inhaling, pull the elbows

and the wrists close to the chest, the beaks pointed out (fig. 5.20j).

12. Exhale using the second healing sound, the kidney sound "Wooooo." As you exhale open the beaks and extend the arms straight down in front of you, the action originating from the shoulders and the heels of the hands leading the way (figs. 5.20k and 5.20l). Spread the fingers wide apart as you extend the arms down.

13. When the arms reach the sides of the hips, lock the elbows and rotate the hands laterally out to each side, keeping the fingers spread apart. Extend the finger tendons, especially at the pinky fingers and the thumbs. Spread the toes, especially the small toes. At the same time, extend the tongue out as far as you can toward the chin (fig. 5.20m). Direct your eyes to look at your nose. Feel the sexual organs pull up as one line to the tongue.

14. Finally, turn the big toes and the heels inward and then move the feet toward one another by taking "steps" that lead with the big toes and follow at the heels, until the feet come together. This will exercise the tendons of the feet.

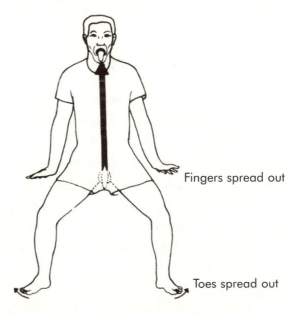

Fingers spread out

Toes spread out

Fig. 5.20m. Sexual organs are connected to the tongue.

15. Repeat the exercise, this time replacing the lung sound in step 7 with the third healing sound, the liver sound "Shhhhhhh." Replace the kidney sound in step 12 with the fourth healing sound, the heart sound "Hawwwwww."

16. Repeat the exercise one more time. At step 7 use the fifth healing sound, the spleen sound "Whoooooo." At step 12 use the sixth healing sound, the triple warmer sound "Heeeeeee." At this point you should feel connected through the legs, spinal tendons, scapulae, and arms.

17. Spread the fingers apart and extend the arms. (Spreading the fingers enlists the use of tendon power.) Feel the force come outward from the scapulae. Relax. Feel chi spread out to all the tendons of the hands, arms, and legs as well as to the tongue.

18. Collect the energy at the navel. Run the energy through the Microcosmic Orbit.

Golden Phoenix Rooting Practices

As you practice these rooting exercises, feel the force transfer from the hand to the ground.

Golden Phoenix Rooting

Practice the Golden Phoenix exercise through step 7. After extending the arms, lock the elbows, lock the wrists, and round the scapulae. Pull up the middle anus and the genital area. Open the knees. Feel that the palms and feet are connected to the ground.

Now have your partner use his or her palms to push your palms. If you are well connected and are relaxing the muscles of the neck, you will feel the force travel to the ground. Remember to relax the muscles of the neck. If you don't you won't be able to transform the force of your partner's weight coming at you.

⟳ The Lift-Up Practice

This exercise requires locking the wrist and hand and feeling connected through the shoulders and scapulae while your partner tries to lift you. Work with a partner who is close to your height. Be cautious because you can be hurt in this practice.

Practice the Golden Phoenix exercise through step 12. Bring the hands to the sides of the thighs. Draw your elbows back, lock the wrists, and round the scapulae, feeling the scapulae's connection with the spinal cord.

Now have your partner put one leg between your legs, his or her palms turned in against your palms. From this stance your partner tries to lift you off the ground (fig. 5.21). Make sure that you lock the elbows, the wrists, and the scapulae; otherwise you can hurt your wrists or scapulae and your partner will be unable to lift you.

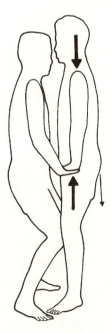

Fig. 5.21. Lift-Up practice

Fig. 5.22. "Beaks" rooting practice

◎ *"Beaks" Rooting Practice*

Practice the Golden Phoenix exercise through step 9. Extend the arms and form beaks, connecting your arms with the scapulae, the spine, the legs, and the feet. Have your partner push your wrists, feeling the force transfer to the ground (fig. 5.22).

Summary: Golden Phoenix Washes Its Feathers

1. Practice lower abdominal breathing in a standing position.
2. Sweep the arms out to your sides.
3. Turn the palms upward.
4. Inhale, raising the hands up along the sides. Pack and wrap the chi into the kidneys, liver, and spleen.
5. Inhale once more, raising the hands higher, and pack and wrap the chi into the lungs and heart.
6. Exhale as you rotate the hands medially. Keeping the perineum and anus closed, push the hands out at shoulder level. Keep the wrists flexed.

7. Inhale and tighten at the perineum and anus. Form beaks with your fingers and pull them in toward the shoulders.
8. Inhale as you pull the beaks closer to your body.
9. Exhale, releasing the perineum and anus and lowering the arms while simultaneously straightening and locking the elbows and knees.
10. When the hands are down with the wrists flexed, turn the hands out to the sides of the thighs and spread the fingers and toes out as much as possible. Thrust the tongue out and pull up the anus and sexual organs.
11. Collect the chi energy at the navel.
12. Practice the Bone Breathing Process.

IRON BRIDGE

The Iron Bridge is designed to strengthen the fascia on the front and back of the body. By stretching the fascia from the pelvis to the neck and on both sides of the rib cage, as you do in this exercise, you greatly increase the flow of chi within the fasciae and tone the musculature.

Arching the spine backward greatly strengthens the lower spine, especially the lumbar region. By stretching the upper back and spine in the opposite direction of its normal curvature, the backbend helps to lessen any forward curvature of the upper back, limber up the shoulder joints, and open the chest. The important point to remember in practicing this exercise is that the bend is from the upper back, not from the hip.

Iron Bridge Standing: Yang Position

In this exercise you will be arching the upper and middle back and stretching the fascia on the front of the body. It is most important to arch the upper and middle back only, not the lumbar spine and hips. Excessive arching of the lower spine and hips can damage the discs between the vertebrae and pinch the nerves that travel through the vertebrae and along the spine. Also, if the arching in the Iron Bridge is mostly from the lower spine there will be much less stretching of the fascia on the front of the body.

To keep the lower spine protected it is necessary to firmly tighten the thighs and buttocks. When you do this you can feel that you are squeezing the sacrum down and reducing the compression in the lower spine.

This position creates a tremendous amount of chi energy that rises up the spine to the head.

1. Stand with the knees straight and the feet 12 inches apart. It is best to position the feet so that they point straight ahead along the second toes. If the toes are turned out there may be unnecessary compression in the lower spine. The thumbs and index fingers touch one another to create an O and the remaining three fingers are held together. Keep the hands straight, low, and slightly in front of the body.

2. Begin abdominal breathing; exhale and flatten the abdomen. Inhale to full capacity. Bend the wrists and elbows to bring the hands up and toward the back; the palms face upward (fig. 5.23). The fingers should reach up toward the scapulae. This will open the sternum, activate the thymus, and stretch the thyroid, the parathyroid, the chest, and the fascia along the sides of the body.

3. Release any accumulated tension in the chest and abdomen. The hips stay over the feet. Tighten the thighs and buttocks to protect the lower back. The knees should be firmly locked and straight.

4. Clench the teeth. Now arch back, initiating the movement at the head. Extend the head back until you can feel the front fascia of the neck stretching. Make sure the head is supported by the muscles of the neck; do not let the head drop back, as this can be quite detrimental to the vertebrae of the neck. If this extension is done properly, you will still feel that the neck is elongating upward even while it is extending back. If you feel any discomfort

Fig. 5.23. The active starting
position for Iron Bridge
yang position

Fig. 5.24. Feel the stretch
of the neck fascia as you
look back.

whatsoever, you are either practicing incorrectly or trying to stretch back too far.

5. Look back, further stretching the fascia at the neck (fig. 5.24). When the front of the neck is stretched properly in this movement you will feel an automatic lifting at the chest, which in turn will stretch the abdomen.

6. As the abdomen stretches, push the pelvis forward, keeping the thighs and buttocks very tight. As you stretch the chest, feel that the breastbone is being pulled forward and up (fig. 5.25).

7. Squeeze the thumb and index fingers together and tighten the muscles of the arms and shoulders. This will stabilize your position. Hold your breath and maintain this position for 30 to 60 seconds.

If this exercise is done properly you will feel the fasciae from the groin up to the chest and the neck pulling tight as a drum without

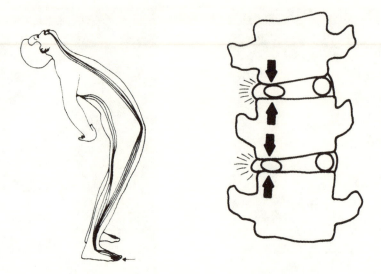

Fig. 5.25. This exercise stretches the fascia up the front of the body. If you arch too far back you are compromising the spine.

having to arch very far back. If you are arching very far back, then you are inevitably overtaxing the lower spine.

If your upper spine is not very flexible or has a large forward curvature, then you may look as though you are hardly arched back at all when you first practice, though you will still be able to feel a stretch across the front of the torso. Remember that, no matter how flexible you are, you will not arch very far back if you are practicing properly. It is a good idea to practice this upper body stretch while sitting until you can do it correctly before practicing in a standing position.

In the beginning have a partner steady you if necessary when you bend backward. If you bend back too far you may fall.

Iron Bridge Resting: Yin Position

1. Exhale as you straighten up and bring the arms to the front. Maintain the Iron Bar hand position as you slowly bend forward from the hip joint. The head is down and the hands are above or touching the ground (fig. 5.26).

Fig. 5.26. Iron Bridge yin position

2. Adjust the tendons, aligning them to the structure. In the beginning do not bend too low; for additional comfort you can slightly bend the knees. If your knees are locked you will experience strain in the knees. If you want to stretch farther forward, do not increase the forward curvature of the upper spine. Instead, stretch forward by lengthening the hamstring muscles at the back of the thighs. If you are stretching forward vigorously, or you are not very limber, bend the knees much more while stretching so that you can lay the entire abdomen firmly on the thighs. Then test your flexibility by slightly straightening the knees while keeping the abdomen on the thighs. Practicing in this way will guarantee that you are only stretching the lower spine and hamstrings, not the upper spine.

3. Feel the chi flow down to the head and then back and down the tongue. The three fingers of each hand are nearly touching each other. Feel the chi flow from the right hand's middle finger to the left hand's middle finger up the left arm to the spine, then to the head and down to the navel.

4. Maintain this position only for as long as you feel comfortable. It is quite strenuous and should be approached with moderation. Stay relaxed until you feel the energy flowing without obstruction. Some people may feel a certain vibration that gradually spreads throughout the body. Allow the vibration to go on for a while. Then slowly stand up to avoid dizziness.

Standing Iron Bridge Rooting Practice

Assume the Iron Bridge posture, then have your partner push you very gently. Remember that the main arch is in the upper back. In the yin position practice, be sure to bend your knees.

Be very careful in these Iron Bridge Rooting Practices. The back and spinal cord are vulnerable to injury in this position. Your partner must be careful to apply pressure very gently to avoid injuring the spinal cord or knocking you off balance.

Yang-Position Rooting Practice

While you are in the backbend position your partner puts one hand on your back and one hand on your chest (fig. 5.27). As your partner slowly presses down, observe that you can take the force only for a few seconds. Bend forward to rest for a while and then practice rooting in the forward position.

Yin-Position Rooting Practice

While you are bent forward have your partner press his or her hands on your spine between your shoulders as you push up from the lower spine (fig. 5.28). Your partner should use his full body weight to press down gently. In this position more force is being exerted on the lower back. This will strengthen the lower spine, especially the lumbar region.

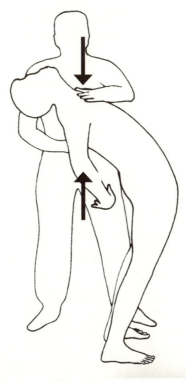

Fig. 5.27. Iron Bridge yang-position rooting

Fig. 5.28. Iron Bridge yin-position rooting

Summary: Iron Bridge

Iron Bridge Standing: Yang Position

1. Stand with knees straight and feet 12 inches apart.
2. Place your hands at the sides of the body. Touch the thumbs and index fingers together, forming a circle with them. The other three fingers of each hand remain straight and touch one other.
3. Begin abdominal breathing. Inhale and arch back from the lower back, keeping the legs straight and the hips aligned over the legs to maintain balance. Bring the hands up and toward the back. Do not overstretch.
4. Push the pelvis forward, keeping thighs and buttocks tight.
5. Squeeze the thumb and index fingers to stabilize your position.

Iron Bridge Resting: Yin Position

1. When you feel you have had enough of the arched yang position, exhale and bring the body slowly to a standing position.
2. Lower your head and bend forward from the hip joint.
3. Bend the knees slightly in the beginning. Relax the arms and allow them to dangle in front of you, maintaining the finger position with the fingers facing each other. Feel the chi flow through each finger. If you can touch the ground, you can feel a certain connection of the chi energy. Breathe normally.
4. Come up very slowly from this position. You may feel dizzy at first.
5. Stand still for a while, collecting the energy. Walk around or lie down on your back and massage your belly from right to left to get your chi circulating.
6. Practice Bone Breathing.
7. Practice the Power Exercise.

IRON BAR

The Iron Bar practice greatly strengthens the front and back fasciae and thus makes the spinal cord very strong. The spinal column consists of twenty-four vertebrae held together by tendons, fascia, and muscles. Normally we do very little to exercise this vital structure. The Iron Bar exercise adjusts the spinal column, strengthening it segment by segment.

 ## Iron Bar Practice

1. Place two chairs facing one another. Have your partner hold the chair at your head to keep it steady. If you do not have a partner, place one of the chairs against a wall.
2. Put both hands palms down behind you on the floor and push yourself up onto the chair. Put the head and shoulders on one chair and the feet and ankles on the other chair. Fold your hands across your belly (fig. 5.29).
3. Straighten the body, especially the low back. Point the toes downward and outward—you will feel a pull on the fascia and tendons. Make sure the lumbar region is straight, not curved. This will help to strengthen the front and back fasciae.

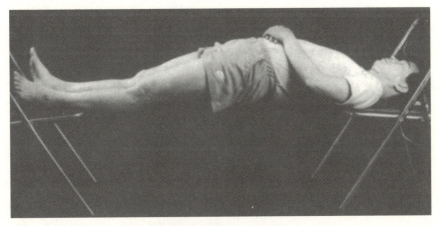

Fig. 5.29. Iron Bar

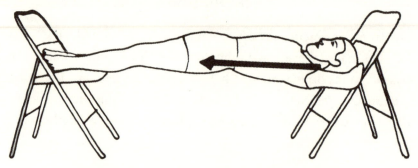

Fig. 5.30. If Iron Bar is too difficult initially, bring your
arms overhead to rest on the chair.

4. If you initially feel that the Iron Bar is too difficult to perform properly and comfortably, bring your arms back over your head onto the chair that your head is on (fig. 5.30). This makes it much easier to maintain a straight spine and is considerably less strenuous. As you feel stronger, gradually increase the amount of force with which you are pushing the arms down into the chair. When you can practice without pushing the arms down at all behind you, you are ready to move gradually to the final position, with the hands resting over the navel.

5. Place both hands on the belly and breathe normally to the abdomen.

6. When you begin to feel uncomfortable, lower your buttocks and feet to the floor, using the hands to steady and hold the chair that the head and shoulders are on. Sit up and place the tongue on the roof of the mouth, letting the energy flow in the Microcosmic Orbit. Do not stand up right away, as you may feel dizzy.

7. In advanced practice you can begin to move the chairs farther apart so that only the neck and head are on the end of the other chair (fig. 5.31). Do not rest the head only, as this can hurt your neck.

This is a very strenuous exercise for the back. Do not attempt to move the chairs farther apart unless you feel very strong. You can

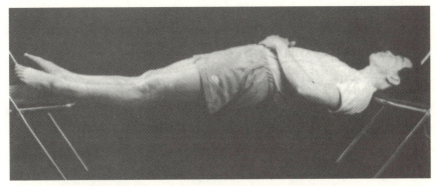

Fig. 5.31. Once you are trained in this position you can move
the chairs farther apart so that only the neck, head, and
heels are resting on the chairs.

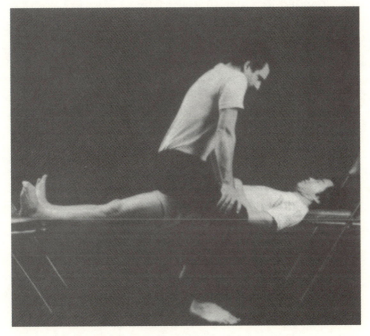

Fig. 5.32. In the advanced practice of the Iron Bar, you can
add weight and still maintain the position.

step up training by supporting a weight on the abdomen. Again, work
gradually. Eventually you will be able to support thirty pounds or
more (fig. 5.32).

Iron Bar Rooting

Have your partner place one hand under your back for support in case you should begin to fall. With the other hand your partner presses down on your abdomen slowly, increasing the pressure gradually.

This exercise strengthens the psoas muscle and the lumbar region of the spine.

Summary: Iron Bar

1. Place two chairs across from one another at an appropriate distance. Place the feet and lower legs on one chair with the toes pointed down and outward, away from you, to develop the most balanced alignment of force in the legs, particularly in the calves.
2. Place both palms down on the floor behind you and lift your head and shoulders on the other chair.
3. Maintain a straight back. To avoid stress in the lower spine while practicing, consciously tighten the buttocks and feel the sacrum squeeze down. This will lengthen the lower spine.
4. Breathe normally from the abdomen.
5. When you are ready, come down to the ground slowly.
6. Stand up and collect the energy at the navel.
7. Practice the Bone Breathing Process.

Structural Alignment and Taoist Yoga*

Radiant health and efficient, powerful movement patterns are possible only when the body's alignment conforms closely to its inherent structural pattern. This ideal pattern is the blueprint for the "stacking" of body segments in space. The function of an appropriate structural relationship is the unhindered flow of energy, breath, alertness, and movement.

The development and use of an aligned structure is basic to Iron Shirt practice. However, for many students it will be difficult to apply principles of alignment in their practice without first approaching structural development in its own right. That is the purpose of this chapter.

The exercises in this chapter lead to actual structural reformation, so that "posturing" yourself according to desirable structural principles becomes easier and more natural. For most of us, "good" posture will remain elusive without undergoing actual structural change. Without intentional practice of good posture, particularly in the beginning, structural reintegration cannot progress.

The anatomical relationships of the entire body, whether moving or stationary, are addressed in these structural exercises. In structural

---

*This chapter was written by Terry Goss, a nutrition, movement, and yoga instructor.

development it is important to conceptually understand what appropriate alignment means. Applying correct structural patterns during your practice of Iron Shirt movements will greatly speed the process of body development.

Remember that these relationships of one body part to another represent an ideal pattern. The more you practice these exercises and apply their principles in daily life, the more closely your own structure will approach the ideal in an increasingly effortless way. There should never be a sense of strain or unpleasantness in trying to "fit" the structural ideal. For most people, simply a month of practice and application will lead to profound improvements in structural health.

As you begin to apply these principles to daily life, there will inevitably be occasional feelings of unnaturalness. This will occur as you choose new patterns of body use that oppose previous distorted patterns that have become habitual. This sense of "artificial posturing" will rapidly decrease with time, if you are practicing diligently. You will then experience ease and naturalness in body usage that allows you to take your Iron Shirt training and respond to a force coming from any direction with an appropriate amount of counterforce. The principle of automatically applying appropriate force is at the heart of martial arts. In order for this full movement potential to be possible, the body must spontaneously return to its "center" of relaxed alignment after movement. This is the relaxed "idling" position that is most unblocked and energetically economical, and out of which graceful movement flows.

Inanimate objects are dominated by the pull of gravity. Plants maintain their uprightness by the rigidity of their cell walls. Animals automatically resist the pull of gravity by normally remaining on a base created by four legs, or by two legs and a strong tail. The upright human being, on the other hand, is a unique expression of evolving self-awareness. The full and intentional expression of standing upright further develops the human spirit. Likewise, the more developed human spirit naturally manifests a greater upright stance. All esoteric traditions that work with energy understand the significance of this fully developed upright human form. This is particularly true of the Taoist tradition.

APPLYING STRUCTURAL ALIGNMENT PRINCIPLES TO IRON SHIRT CHI KUNG PRACTICE

Diligent practice of Iron Shirt Chi Kung will lead to increased flexibility and range of motion at the spine and other joints. As the body becomes more open, it is important to understand and apply the principles of healthy structural alignment in daily life. Since many of us have come from a background of structural randomness and distortion, it is necessary to learn what to do with our various body segments as our body becomes open and capable of new, more appropriate alignment. In effect, we must learn how best to "wear" the body.

The very center of our physical structure is the spine and its foundation, the pelvis. Encased within the spine and cranium is the central nervous system, the center of our conscious life; thus, structural health of the spine is the foundation for the structural and energetic health of the rest of the body. The basic structural exercises taught in this section focus strongly on the spine. Regular practice of these exercises will help heal any existing structural problems and tremendously enhance your Iron Shirt practice.

The structural exercises that follow—Structural Training against a Wall, Spinal Elongation Breathing, Door Hanging, Shoulder Widening, and Backbend—develop a straighter, more elongated spine and joint spaces that are not cramped. The spine will retain its three normal curves, but these curves will not be as excessive as they are in most of the rest of the population. Attention to details will guarantee that your practice is safe, effective, and progressive. Also described are additional exercises, such as the two variations of Warrior Pose, that complement the practice of Iron Shirt Chi Kung by eliminating structural blocks in the hips and back and by strengthening the lower body.

By applying the structural principles during your Iron Shirt practice, as well as in your daily life, you will come to feel the primary forces that are always acting on your structure. These two basic forces are a strong downward rooting force connecting you to the ground; and, at the same time, a strong upward elongating force lengthening your spine that connects you to the heavens. To attain balance and integration, both of these forces must be developed.

RELAXATION TIPS

For the Lower Abdomen

At the level of the navel and the Door of Life (located behind the navel), rooting and elongating forces originate and mingle. For this mingling to fully occur, the lower abdomen must always remain relaxed. The lower abdomen should remain soft, except when you are making a full exhalation, such as when you are very active or practicing abdominal breathing. The rest of the time (which is most of the time), practice releasing any tension in the lower abdomen until this becomes automatic. Your breathing, digestion, and elimination will improve, and the rest of your body will relax more fully.

The two central points of the body that reflect and determine your daily tension level are your face and your lower abdomen. During your daily activities, practice smiling with the eyes and face and keeping your lower abdomen relaxed. Remember always to relax as much as possible, no matter what you are doing. You will feel much happier, your organs will function better, and your energy will flow more easily.

For the Inner Smile

While practicing these structural alignment exercises, also practice the Inner Smile. If you can maintain the Inner Smile while practicing vigorous exercises such as Iron Shirt and Warrior Pose, you will be able to maintain the Inner Smile easily during times of emotional challenge as well. Remember that the face is not only the primary expressor of body language; your face also returns to your system the very emotions it expresses outwardly.

Whenever you exercise, intentionally develop the various details of facial alignment that accompany soft, relaxed, smiling eyes. You will gain much more energy and emotional balance from your practice.

When you practice the Inner Smile, let all of the facial muscles relax. This relaxation can be seen and felt particularly around the eyes and mouth. Feel the eyelids close slightly and gently as the area around the eyes relaxes and the space between the eyebrows widens. Let the eyes be receptive to incoming visual stimuli. Rather than grasping for sights and sounds, let them flow into their respective organs. Allow the nostrils and sinuses to subtly widen, creating more space for the breath to enter the body. Let the outer corners of the mouth lift gently with the tongue up to the palate, the lips slightly touching, and the jaws just separated or barely touching. This will produce a smile like that of the Mona Lisa or Buddha. This lifting of the corners of the mouth should be effortless, the outer result of an inner smile (fig. 6.1).

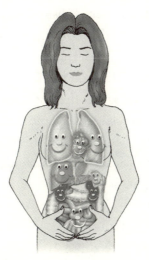

Fig. 6.1. The Inner Smile

If you can relax deeply enough, all of these details will take place spontaneously because they are natural aspects of healthy facial alignment in a happy, centered person. Practicing them intentionally will quickly condition them into your basic neuromuscular patterns. Practice the Inner Smile in this way with your eyes open as well as closed. This will enable you to apply it at all times. A smile in the eyes and the subtle lift at the outer corners of the mouth are the most important details. Whenever you do this it will be easy to have access to feelings of inner happiness, serenity, and compassion.

Feeling the Inner Smile and relaxed facial alignment during Iron Shirt will ensure that the mind remains more centered and calm, and that you are continuous and fluid in your movement. As a result, you can experience and develop the flow of chi.

For Tight Jaw Muscles

Chronically tight jaw muscles are not uncommon in our culture. Tight jaw muscles often distort the entire facial structure. Clenched or tightened jaws become that way for various reasons. Strong emotions that are held back from being expressed may produce this effect. On the other hand, the universal distortion of a collapsed neck, in which the chin moves forward out of alignment, will often cause compensations in the jaw pattern. Whatever the cause, tight jaw muscles need to be loosened up so that you can fully practice the Inner Smile and relax completely throughout the body.

Since it is difficult to relax the jaw muscles simply through intention, an exercise using a cork can help. This is a beneficial exercise for people who have a lot of jaw tension, although practically everyone can benefit from trying it.

Take a cork and cut it, if necessary, to make it fit between the front teeth when your mouth is wide open without strain (fig. 6.2). Hold the cork between the teeth for 10 minutes every day for several weeks. As the jaw muscles stretch open, use a longer cork until you can easily use a normal-sized one.

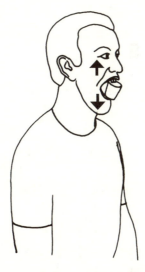

Fig. 6.2. Stretching tight jaw muscles

This exercise can be done while reading, driving, showering, or watching TV. Do not do this if it produces pain, if your jaws make audible sounds when they open and close, or if you have a history of jaw dislocation or other such problems.

STRUCTURAL TRAINING AGAINST A WALL

Using a wall for feedback, you will be able to feel when you have a structurally aligned, elongated spine. This exercise is dependent only upon a wall or door to lean against, so it can be done anywhere as a postural recharging exercise. It is a powerful method for decompressing the vertebrae and lessening discomfort for those with back problems, particularly low back pain and sciatica.

Lower Body

Lean against a wall with the heels approximately 12 to 18 inches from the wall (fig. 6.3). Bend the knees and tuck the pelvis so that the

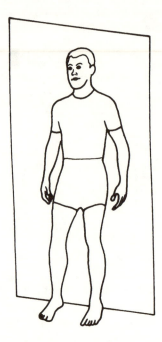

Fig. 6.3. The position for Structural Training against a Wall

lower spine is flattened to the wall without discomfort. Work into this position gradually if you feel discomfort initially. The calves will be perpendicular to the ground or slightly angled back toward the wall. You should feel that you are comfortably leaning against the wall.

Feet

Press the balls of the big toes firmly to the floor, then widen the feet across the balls. This will spread the toes. Now equalize the weight between the ball of the big toe, the last two toes, and the middle of the heel. The toes should remain relaxed without grasping the floor, with the second toes pointing straight ahead. Keep the feet aligned in this way, even if you feel pigeon toed. Apply this same foot alignment when standing, walking, or exercising.

Head, Neck, and Upper Back

Bring as much of the upper back as flat to the wall as possible without strain (fig. 6.4). Begin with the sacrum against the wall while holding the remainder of the spine rounded forward away from the wall. Now roll the spine vertebra by vertebra against the wall until you reach your limit of flexibility. Hold the head as if it is gently pushed back from the upper lip and lifted (or suspended) from its crown. Do not overdo this by tucking the chin. For many people the back of the head will not touch the wall.

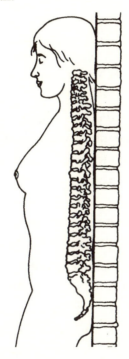

Fig. 6.4 Bring as much of the upper back flat to the wall as possible.

Arms/Shoulders

Tuck the shoulders down away from the ears and widen them out to the sides (fig. 6.5). See the Shoulder Widening Exercise in this chapter.

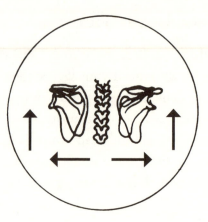

Fig. 6.5. Widen the shoulders away from the spine.

There are several possible arm positions:

1. Simply let the arms hang relaxed at the sides with the palms facing into the torso. This is the most natural position and is appropriate if you are practicing around other people (at work, for example) and do not want to look like you are doing an "exercise."
2. Starting from that position, bring the elbows back to barely touch the wall without touching the forearms or grossly changing the position of the shoulders. As you bring the elbows back to the wall the shoulders will naturally roll back, but only slightly. This position helps to properly align the shoulders.
3. Roll the left shoulder blade away from the wall until only the inner edge of the left shoulder blade is touching the wall. Now roll the rest of the left shoulder blade back to touch the wall. Repeat on the right side, then bring the arms to position 1 or 2. This position strongly stretches the shoulders out to either side and thus widens the upper back and chest. This stretch is good preparation for the Iron Shirt postures that require scapulae power.

Do not attempt positions 2 or 3 unless they can be done without strain.

Stretching the Lower Spine

For additional stretch in the lower back, bend the knees and sink down lower on the wall. Now, keeping the sacrum in firm contact with the wall, slowly straighten the knees back to the original position. For even more stretch, place the hands around the hips and push down while you straighten back to the original position. This will strongly lengthen the lower spine. Do not attempt this until the lower back can be brought to the wall without discomfort.

Simply standing in the Structural Training against a Wall position will help to decompress and straighten the spine. It is not necessary to do special breathing exercises in order to derive benefit from this position. The goal is to have a straightening spine, not a straight spine. The wall gives you feedback when your spine is in a more straightened alignment.

In a structurally balanced body, breathing causes a natural elongation of the spine. This occurs to the greatest degree when the chest is filled during inhalation. The lifting and widening of the ribs causes the vertebrae to separate from each other and the spine to lengthen. Practicing deep chest breathing in this position and in Door Hanging leads to a conditioning of this natural breath/alignment relationship (fig. 6.6). Once you have developed this spinal elongation it will occur even in your more relaxed, daily-life breathing—which is primarily abdominal breathing. This opening and closing of the spine with breathing is an integral part of the normal body mechanism that pumps blood, chi, and cerebrospinal fluid around the central nervous system.

Spinal Elongation Breathing

To enhance the effects of Structural Training against a Wall and the use of the breath, first exhale fully. Then, inhale slowly and deeply through the nose, directing the breath up into the chest. The abdomen should remain flat. As you inhale, visualize and feel the spine

Fig. 6.6. Stretching the spine and breathing for spinal elongation

lengthening. This will happen automatically if you stay relaxed. Do not try too hard. Once you feel spinal elongation, you can further refine this sense by feeling a wave of elongation starting at the base of the spine and traveling upward as you inhale.

As you exhale, continue to feel yourself lengthening upward. You will feel the structural muscles around the spine take over. The lengthening upward that occurs with exhalation is more subtle than that which occurs with inhalation, and is really a wave of support that prevents excessive collapse. This wave of support begins at the head and travels downward as you exhale.

Breathe into the chest without intentional abdominal contraction or unintentional abdominal expansion. Because of structural blockages in the chest it may be necessary at first to tighten the abdominal muscles in order to direct the breath into the chest. Breathing into the chest in this way is meant to release structural blockages in the chest and lengthen the spine fully.

Do this if necessary; otherwise the abdomen will protrude as you inhale, with very little expansion in the chest. Over time, gradually use less and less force to hold the abdomen in while inhaling.

When you finish practicing forget about your breathing and let it flow naturally. Natural breathing begins in the abdomen and only expands the chest when you are very active and thus breathing fully. Do not maintain chest breathing in your daily activities or you may cause energy to congest in the chest and head.

HEAD AND NECK ALIGNMENT AS THE BASIS FOR SPINAL ELONGATION AND UPRIGHT STRUCTURE

Spinal Elongation Breathing cannot lengthen the spine unless the head is held as if it is pushed back from the upper lip and lifted from its crown without strain (fig. 6.7). If the chin moves slightly forward and up, the neck collapses and the entire upper body will be collapsed and distorted. Then the spine will curve excessively and no type of deep, free breathing will be possible. Even the windpipe itself becomes constricted. This is the condition of most people's necks. It is rare to find people in our culture who do not have chronic misalignment of the neck vertebrae for this very reason.

The feeling that the head is suspended from its crown and gently pushed back from the upper lip without strain should be applied at all times. It is the foundation for an erect upper body and free breathing. Appropriate alignment of the head and neck ensures healthy communication between the body and head. With this healthy communication, awareness spreads more fully to the whole body.

In a higher meditation formula of the Universal Tao system called Lesser Enlightenment of the Kan and Li one learns to observe oneself with the inner eye. In the body structure, consciously aligning the

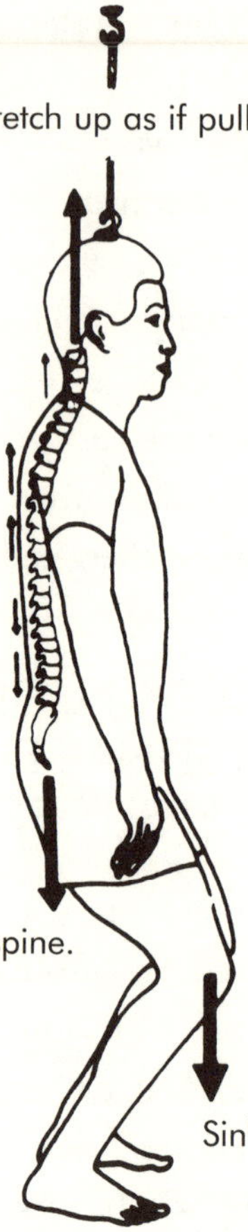

Push back from the upper lip and lift the head as if from its crown.

Feel the head stretch up as if pulled by a string.

Feel the sacrum pull down the spine.

Sink the knees down.

Fig. 6.7. Proper alignment of the head and neck is the basis for effective spinal elongation and an upright structure.

head and neck without strain is the foundation for a greater awareness that results from self-observation and self-awareness. In the practice of hatha yoga, elongation of the back of the neck that results from head and neck alignment is called "the root of watchfulness" or "the root of mindfulness."

Even after balanced structural alignment becomes easy and natural, a very subtle intention to maintain head/neck alignment may be necessary. This slight lifting and moving back of the head is the single most important factor in making the entire body erect and elongated. The actual elongation and shifting back of the head is often only a very small change. Without it, however, the chest, upper back, and entire spine cannot come into alignment. This importance is due to the fact that the neck and head are the upper end of the column that we wish to lift. The importance of this one factor of neck and head alignment cannot be overstressed. Whole body integration is not possible without it.

It is useful to be familiar with the feeling of neck collapse that afflicts nearly everyone. After aligning the body, let the chin move forward and up and thus out of alignment. Notice how the back of the neck shortens, the throat closes, the sternum sinks, the chest closes, the upper back arches excessively, the shoulders roll forward, breathing is restricted, and spinal elongation becomes impossible. Then practice a Spinal Elongation breath as the head is once again placed appropriately and feel the sense of full openness that accompanies it throughout the body.

Greater self-awareness, full uprightness of the trunk, and unstrained alignment of the head and neck are integrally related. The interplay of these three factors is particularly evident in Iron Shirt. The intention required to maintain head/neck alignment and the other aspects of a fully aligned structure is an expression of the autonomous will of a self-aware being. Likewise, relaxed practice of fully aligning oneself develops this autonomous will in a beneficial way.

Door Hanging

Developing a straighter, more elongated spine is the purpose of both Door Hanging and Structural Training against a Wall. In Door Hanging, however, the arms are held over the head, which tractions the spine and greatly increases spinal lengthening. Daily practice of Door Hanging for even a few weeks will lead to better posture, a more flexible spine, reduction of chronic back stress, and a heightened awareness of natural structural alignment. Door Hanging will also help you to be aware of and control your psoas muscles, which are vital to many Universal Tao practices.

Roll a towel and place it over the top of a door. Lean against the narrow edge of the door, bringing the spine as flat to the edge as possible without discomfort (fig. 6.8). Follow all position details for Structural Training against a Wall, except those for the arms.

Maintain your attention at the lower ribs and the middle and lower spine. Bring the arms overhead without letting the spine come away from the edge of the door. Feel that you are tucking the lower ribs in as the arms are brought overhead.

Grasp the towel fairly high but keep the elbows somewhat bent. Continue to pull the shoulders down strongly and widen the shoul-

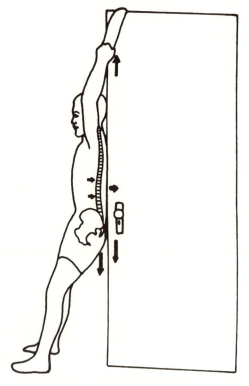

Fig. 6.8. Door Hanging

ders to the sides. Do not hang from the towel. All of the body weight is still on the legs. If the shoulders are strained in this position, hold the towel lower to decrease the shoulder stretch. If necessary the elbows may be only shoulder height or even lower.

If a towel is not long enough for you, use a thick rope. Gradually you will be able to hold the towel higher as your shoulder joints become more flexible. The first position of the Backbend exercise (detailed later in this chapter) will help limber your shoulder joints.

While maintaining this position, practice breathing up into the chest, as in Spinal Elongation Breathing or Structural Training against a Wall. Along with the traction of the arms overhead, filling the chest during inhalation will result in tremendous elongation of the spine. It will not take much practice to feel your spine begin to lengthen. As you feel this happen, after every five breaths or so, bring the pelvis and the lower and middle spine a few inches away from the door edge. This allows the upper spine to lengthen further down the door. Again, bring the spine and pelvis back to the door edge and continue practicing.

If possible, practice from 1 to 3 minutes or longer. Do not continue if discomfort arises. Straining will not open your spine faster; it will add more tightness. Regular practice and respecting your own limits will inevitably lead to rapid spinal elongation and realignment.

To leave the Door Hanging position, walk the feet back toward the door and stand straight up. Do not come up by pushing the pelvis away from the door first.

When you are completely comfortable with the exercise described above, you can practice Full Hanging by letting your full body weight hang from the towel. Gradually bend the knees and slide down the door edge until the arms are straight and holding you up entirely. All other details of practice are the same. Hold this for as long as comfortable, which may only be a few seconds, then come up. Be sure to continue stabilizing the shoulders by feeling them pull down and widen to the sides.

Full Hanging is very strengthening and produces tremendous spinal extension, but must not be attempted if it causes strain.

FEELING AND USING THE PSOAS MUSCLES

Once you feel comfortable with the details of Door Hanging, consciously relax the abdominal wall while you practice. As you soften the abdominal muscles, relax and straighten the spine against the door edge. You will be able to feel a sensation of pulling in and up deep inside behind the front lower ribs. This is the left and right psoas muscles at work (fig. 6.9).

Feel this same sensation of pulling in and up deep inside behind the front lower ribs when you walk and sit. This will keep your lower

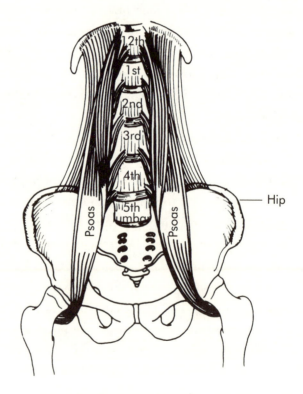

Fig. 6.9. The psoas muscles

spine lengthened and comfortable without needing to "suck your gut." Pulling the abdomen in to flatten the belly or straighten the lower spine will hamper your energy flow and organ function. On the other hand, working the psoas properly will not only align the lower spine but will also flatten the belly without tightening it.

When you carry the head as if gently pushed back from the upper lip and suspended from its crown, the tendency is to let the lower ribs push forward. To prevent this, feel that you are tucking the lower ribs back slightly. Tuck the lower ribs from inside, not from tightening the abdomen. This will put you in touch with proper psoas alignment. You are not actually sinking the lower ribs back, for this would cause you to slouch. You are instead positioning the ribs in a straight line, with the abdomen below and the chest above. Feeling the tucking sensation will stabilize the mid-torso and allow the whole spine to lengthen equally. The feeling, once it is developed, is that there is a subtle pulling back and up deep inside at the lower rib area. Experience this first in Door Hanging, then apply it at all times. Like all structural improvements, intention is required initially. Gradually the new posture will become automatic.

Door Hanging is the key to developing this psoas feeling. If the spine remains on the door and the abdomen is soft, then you need only relax and gradually sense what is already happening inside. It also helps to have a good mental picture of the anatomy involved. Once you have developed this psoas feeling you will find how important it is in all of the Universal Tao practices. During your practice of Iron Shirt, when you are using reverse breathing to pack the abdomen, slightly increase the psoas work of pulling in and up behind the front lower ribs. This will allow you to pack even more fully but without tightening the abdominal wall to do it. Gradually you will be able to pack very powerfully with very little abdominal tension at all. When you thrust back at T11 to pack the lower back, apply the psoas work and you will be able to focus your force to the T11 area much more directly.

The Psoas Muscles and the Six Healing Sounds

The relationship between the psoas alignment and the lower area can be felt very well when practicing the Six Healing Sounds. (For detailed information on the Six Healing Sounds, see the book *Taoist Ways to Transform Stress into Vitality*.) Remember to keep the lower rib area back using the psoas muscles, not by tightening the abdomen. For the lung, liver, and heart sounds, be sure to keep the lower ribs held in. Then, while exhaling and making the unvoiced sound, you can put pressure within each organ more effectively. While exhaling, continuously increase the pressure to the particular organ area. At this point you will feel that you are "wringing out" the stale energy from each organ with this pressure.

Using the correct psoas alignment as you inhale will allow you to more easily direct the fresh energy from your breath into the organ. When doing the liver sound, tilt to the right and slightly forward from the lower rib area. This will increase the pressure you can apply to the liver. For the heart sound, tilt to the left and slightly forward and stretch the heart meridian by stretching the little finger. For the lung sound, stretch the lung meridian by stretching the thumb.

For the kidney and spleen sounds, the lower ribs should sink back so that you can apply pressure in each organ. When the lower ribs sink back you are really accentuating the psoas stretch.

Using the psoas muscles correctly will improve your practice of the Six Healing Sounds. By simply practicing the Six Healing Sounds you will become aware of the psoas alignment, particularly when the arms are overhead.

Standing Pelvic Alignment

Balanced alignment of the psoas muscles is also essential for correct leg movement and pelvic alignment. However the feet are placed, be sure that the pelvis is not tilted back or pushed to one side. The knees should remain at least slightly bent and the arches of the feet lifted by distributing the weight equally on the three corners of each foot.

When the pelvis is askew or the knees are locked back there is stress in the lower back and knees; integration between the lower and upper halves of the body becomes impossible. For most people, maintaining structural alignment in the lower body while "standing around" requires intention. This is due to weakness in the legs and buttocks. Maintaining an aligned stance during daily life will do a great deal to strengthen the lower body, improve energetic flow, and heal lower back problems.

Seated Pelvic Alignment

When you sit erect for meditation, be sure that the sitz bones are directed straight down into the chair seat. Tucking the chin slightly will align your spine and give a gentle pull to the spinal cord. Then energy will flow more easily into the back portion of the Microcosmic Orbit. If you find that placing your hands in your lap causes your shoulders to roll forward or your upper back to become uncomfortable, place your hands on a thin cushion or folded blanket in your lap (fig. 6.10). When your chi flow is strong, this will no longer be a problem.

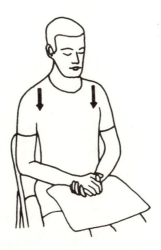

Fig. 6.10. Practice circulating chi through the Microcosmic Orbit while in a sitting position.

SHOULDER WIDENING

The Shoulder Widening exercise develops natural alignment of the shoulders by widening the shoulder blades out to the sides. In all body segments, healthy alignment leads to an increase of space. When the shoulders are pulled back, the width of the upper back is decreased and the upper spine is compressed. When the shoulders are rolled forward, the chest collapses and its width is decreased. However, when the shoulders are dropped down and widened out to the sides, there is an equal opening of space across both the front and back of the upper torso.

In several of the Iron Shirt exercises, flexibility and control are developed by widening the shoulder blades out to the sides. You feel the chest sink, but not collapse, and the shoulders drop down. This movement creates the necessary connection to the rib cage, which will permit the chi energy to flow, thus giving the practitioner scapulae power. After your Iron Shirt practice remember to let the shoulders return to a natural "idling" position—dropped and widened out to the sides. Do not permit the shoulders to roll forward at all so that there will be no significant loss of potential scapulae power.

Shoulder Widening Exercise

You can practice while sitting, standing, or in Structural Alignment against a Wall. Be sure that the spine is erect. Aligned placement of the shoulders must begin with an erect neck and head and an erect upper back and chest.

Hold each wrist with the opposite hand. Keep the arms down low at the torso. Gently but firmly pull the elbows out to the sides without letting go of the hands. Be sure the shoulders are kept consciously dropped. Let the force at the elbows be reflected up to the shoulder joints, which will increase the sense of widening at the shoulders (fig. 6.11). This is a subtle feeling but can very definitely be recognized.

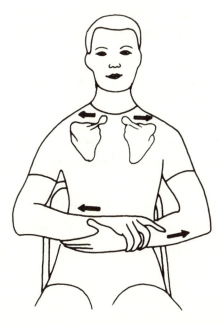

Fig. 6.11. Shoulder Widening exercise

Slowly release the pulling out of the elbows and the active drop-ping and widening of the shoulders. Maintain the same dropped and widened position of the shoulders, which are now in a relaxed state with the arms hanging loosely at your sides.

If your shoulders are usually rolled forward, you will also need to roll them back while performing this exercise. Be sure not to roll them back so far that the shoulder blades begin to move toward each other.

While practicing this exercise feel which muscles are doing the work of active shoulder alignment. Muscles in both the chest and back will be working. Then, after mastering the exercise as outlined above, begin to practice actively aligning the shoulders while the arms remain at your sides. You will be able to align the entire upper body easily and quickly whenever you wish. Be sure to maintain the drop-ping and widening of the shoulders, even when you raise the arms above shoulder height. This stabilizes the shoulders and makes arm movement steadier and more grounded while lessening the build-up of tension in the shoulders and neck.

BALANCING THE CURVES OF THE SPINE

The Backbend stretches the upper back and spine opposite to the normal direction of its curve. This helps lessen the often excessive forward curve of the upper back, limbers up the shoulder joints, and opens the chest.

The Backbend is the most important stretch for a healthy upper spine and freer breathing pattern. The Backbend is also very good preparation for the Iron Bridge Iron Shirt Chi Kung posture.

Backbend

Roll a blanket tightly and place it on the floor. Lie over the blanket so that it is just below the top of the shoulders. Lengthen the spine by tucking the pelvis to straighten the lower spine. Tuck the chin in to lengthen the back of the neck (fig. 6.12). If you feel any discomfort in the back, the blanket is too high on the spine.

If there is any discomfort in the neck after tucking in the chin and elongating the back of the neck, it is essential that you place the head on another blanket or cushion. This extra neck support should

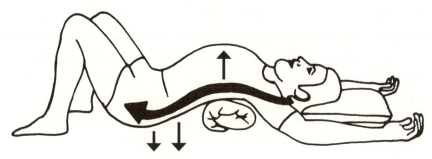

Fig. 6.12. The position of the back during a backbend

be lower than the support under your back but high enough to eliminate any neck strain and allow you to feel that the back of the neck is lengthening.

As you practice over time and gradually increase the height of the rolled-up blanket, it may be necessary to use a neck support. This is particularly true in the first position, when the blanket is just below the top of the shoulders.

Slowly bring the arms back to rest on the floor above the head, with the elbows well bent. Only do this if you can accomplish it without strain. If bringing the arms back causes discomfort they can remain at the sides or be brought back only so far as produces stretch without strain. If brought back only part way the arms can either be held there or placed on a cushion, a piece of furniture, or another prop. As the shoulder joints become more limber the arms can be brought lower. Be sure to continue keeping the shoulder blades dropped and widened as the arms are brought back.

While relaxing in this Backbend posture breathe deeply and slowly, directing the breath to fill the chest rather than expand the abdomen. This greatly increases the stretch of the spine and chest. If necessary, hold the abdomen in while inhaling so that chest expansion can occur. It may seem difficult initially to breathe up into the chest while practicing the Backbend, but practice will be rewarded by a great deal of structural opening in the chest and upper back.

In order to limber up the whole upper spine and shoulder joints, practice the Backbend in each of the following positions. Do not practice with the blanket below the sternum.

- First position: The blanket is just under the tops of the shoulders.
- Second position: The blanket is under the middle of the chest.
- Third position: The blanket is under the sternum.

Remain in each position for several minutes, more if you are comfortable. Most people find the Backbend very pleasant from the beginning: it is similar to receiving a back massage. If the Backbend is initially a difficult stretch for you, leave the position and rest before continuing to the next position. Once the Backbend is easy and pleasant you can shift from first to second to third positions on the blanket without coming up first.

To get up out of the Backbend, use your hand to lift your head to a chin-on-chest position, then roll off the blanket to one side before sitting up. This will prevent strain on the neck or back.

Once you come to sitting, bend forward and relax after the Backbend, as you do upon completion of the Iron Bridge. The knees should be at least slightly bent. If the knees are locked they will be strained. If you want to stretch farther forward, do not increase the forward curvature of the upper spine. Instead, stretch forward by letting the hamstring muscles at the backs of the thighs lengthen.

If you are stretching forward vigorously, or if you are not very limber, bend the knees much more while stretching so that you can lay the whole abdomen firmly on the thighs. Then challenge your flexibility by slightly straightening the knees while keeping the abdomen on the thighs. Practicing in this way will guarantee that you are only stretching the lower spine and hamstrings, not arching the upper spine.

As the upper back becomes more limber, continue to increase the height of the blanket(s) in order to feel a strong stretch with no discomfort.

STRENGTHENING THE BUTTOCKS AND LOWER LEGS

Practicing the yoga posture Warrior Poses leads to great flexibility and strength in the buttocks and legs. As strength and flexibility develop there is structural opening and realigning in the hip/thigh/lower back area that is essential in Iron Shirt. The awareness created in Warrior Pose develops the ability to use the lower body in movement or in standing without compressing the lower spine or neck.

Warrior 1 Pose

Stand with the left foot straight ahead and the right foot turned in 45 degrees. A line through the middle of the left heel should intersect the middle of the arch of the right foot. Throughout the exercise keep equal weight on the three points of each foot. The distance between the two feet should be as wide as possible without losing the indicated alignment for the low back and back leg.

Begin with both legs straight at the knees. Strongly turn the pelvis under so that the lumbar spine is straight. This will require strong work from the buttocks. It is absolutely essential that the low back remains in this straightened position throughout the exercise; if the feet are too far apart it will be impossible to keep the pelvis tucked under.

After flattening the lower spine, extend upward through the whole spine. Hold the head as if it is gently pushed back from the upper lip and lifted from its crown. Do not permit the lower rib area to push forward. This is particularly true in these Warrior Poses, and more so in Warrior 2 Pose than in Warrior 1 Pose. Maintain a full extension of the spine throughout the exercise.

Now exhale and bend the left (front) leg until the left knee is directly over the left ankle, keeping the right (back) leg as straight as possible (fig. 6.13). Do not let the left knee move to the right as it comes forward. This would prevent the groin from opening. The knee must remain positioned over the ankle.

If the feet are too far apart you will not be able to bend the left knee all the way over the left ankle without arching the lower spine and/or bending the back leg a lot at the knee.

It is all right to let the back leg bend a little to keep the lower spine straight. As you are holding the position, gradually straighten the back leg more at the knee until you reach your limit. Do not straighten it to the point where your lower spine begins to arch.

Maintain this position for 1 to 2 minutes, breathing slowly and deeply up into the chest to elongate the spine. Breathe continuously without any pause.

Fig. 6.13. Warrior 1 Pose

Come out of the position while exhaling by first straightening the front leg and then turning to bring the feet parallel to one another. Now bring the feet together.

Repeat on the other side.

Warrior 2 Pose

Stand with both feet facing straight ahead, the right foot several feet behind the left foot and several inches to the right. Lift the heel of the right foot off the floor. Throughout the exercise keep equal weight on the three points of the left (front) foot and equal weight across the balls of the right (back) foot. The distance between the two feet should be as wide as possible without losing the indicated alignment for the low back and back leg.

Turn the pelvis so that the pelvis and torso are square with the front thigh. The navel will be pointing in the direction of the front foot. Begin with both knees straight. Strongly turn the pelvis under so that the lumbar spine is straight. It is absolutely essential that the low back remains unarched throughout the exercise. If the feet are too far apart, this will be impossible.

The next steps are exactly the same as in Warrior 1 Pose.

After flattening the lower spine, extend upward through the whole spine. Hold the head as if it is gently pushed back from the upper lip and lifted from its crown. Do not permit the lower rib area to push forward. This is particularly true in these Warrior Poses, and more so in Warrior 2 Pose than in Warrior 1 Pose. Maintain a full extension of the spine throughout the exercise.

Now exhale and bend the left (front) leg until the left knee is directly over the left ankle, keeping the right (back) leg as straight as possible. Do not let the left knee move to the right as it comes forward. This would prevent the groin from opening. The knee must remain positioned over the ankle.

If the feet are too far apart you will not be able to bend the left knee all the way over the left ankle without arching the lower spine and/or bending the back leg a lot at the knee.

It is all right to let the back leg bend a little to keep the lower spine straight. As you are holding the position, gradually straighten the back leg more at the knee until you reach your limit. Do not straighten it to the point where your lower spine begins to arch.

Maintain this position for 1 to 2 minutes, breathing slowly and deeply up into the chest to elongate the spine. Breathe continuously without any pause.

When your practice has become familiar and strong, add the following arm position. Extend both arms straight up, keeping the shoulder blades dropped and widened; the palms face each other (fig. 6.14, page 224). Pay particular attention to the lower rib area, preventing it from extending forward as the arms are extended upward.

Because this is a strengthening exercise, it requires strong concentration and strong (but not stressful) exertion to maintain the straight lower spine and the straightening of the back leg. When first learning Warrior Pose it is usually best to use the arms to aid pelvic alignment. One hand pushes the sacrum down and forward from the back while the other hand pushes in and slightly up at the lower ribs from the front (fig. 6.15). This helps greatly in keeping the spine straight, and you can keep all of your concentration on the lower body exertion.

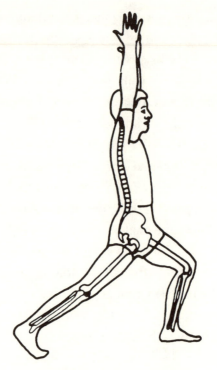

Fig. 6.14. Warrior 2 Pose

Fig. 6.15. Arm position for beginners

If you practice Warrior Pose two or three times per week, strength will develop rapidly and flexibility will develop slowly but steadily. As flexibility increases the feet can be held farther apart until finally the front thigh will be parallel to the floor while the other details of the form are maintained.

This final position requires tremendous flexibility and strength. Most people will not achieve this for a long time. Just remember that an arched low back or well-bent back knee means the feet are too far apart. It is a good idea to check your lower back in a mirror when first learning. You may be quite surprised how close the feet have to be positioned to practice properly.

Finally, when your practice has become familiar and strong, add the following arms position. Extend both arms strongly at shoulder height directly to the front and back. Let the eyes gaze at the tip of the second finger of the forward arm. Keep the shoulders pulled down rather than hunched. Extend from the fingertips through each joint to the shoulder blades.

Iron Shirt Body Construction

This chapter is concerned with the construction of the fascia and its structural interrelationship with bones, muscles, and tendons. Instruction on the muscle-tendon meridians of the body increases awareness of the body's construction. That awareness is vital to the work at hand: the creation and storage of chi energy and its circulation throughout the body. Dr. Michael Posner, a practicing chiropractor, provides an introduction to this chapter by discussing the major keys to good health through an understanding of body structure.

Learn as much as you can about the way that you are constructed because it will speed your progress in the martial arts. Knowing what makes you tick and how you are put together is important in putting you in contact with yourself through Iron Shirt Chi Kung.

IRON SHIRT AND CHIROPRACTIC*

Among all health professions nowadays, one thing that is commonly considered detrimental to our health is the phenomenon of stress. Various methodologies and theories have emerged that aim to help minimize the amount of stress a person has to cope with. I wish to

---

* This section of the chapter was written by Michael Posner, D.C.

discuss the unavoidable stress of gravity on a body's structure when in an upright position, some health implications of that particular stressor, and how, through proper alignment of bone structure, we can efficiently minimize stress and increase good health.

As gravitational forces act upon our bodies when we are upright, various groups of musculature work so that we can stay erect. To resist gravity these muscles must exert a certain amount of energy. These antigravity muscles help to stabilize the bone structure in such a way that movement is possible in an upright position. The success that a person has in meeting the constant stress of gravity may have a subtle yet profound influence on his or her health, performance, and emotional states.

It is necessary to understand some basic concepts, such as line of gravity and center of gravity, as they relate to our bodies' structures.

When viewed laterally, the body's line of gravity falls from above down through the earlobe; slightly behind the mastoid process; through the ondontoid process, a toothlike projection from the body of the axis (the second vertebra of the neck) upon which the first cervical vertebra rotates; and through the middle of the shoulder joint (fig. 7.1). It touches the midpoint of the frontal borders of T2 and T12, then falls just slightly outside to the sacrum, slightly behind the axis of the hip joint, slightly behind to the patella (or kneecap), crosses in front to the middle malleolus (the hammer-shaped bone on each side of the ankle), and through the outer bone of the ankle to fall between the heel and metatarsal heads. When viewed from the back the line of gravity passes through the occipital bone at the lower back part of the skull, C7 and L5, the coccyx and pubic cartilage (the supporting tissue of the pubic bones), and bisects the knees and ankles.

Because gravity acts on all parts of the body, a person's entire weight can be considered to be concentrated at a point where the gravitational pull on one side of the body is equal to the pull on the other side of the body. This point is the body's center of gravity. Generally speaking, the center of gravity is located in a region directly in front of and about $1^1/_2$ inches above and below the level

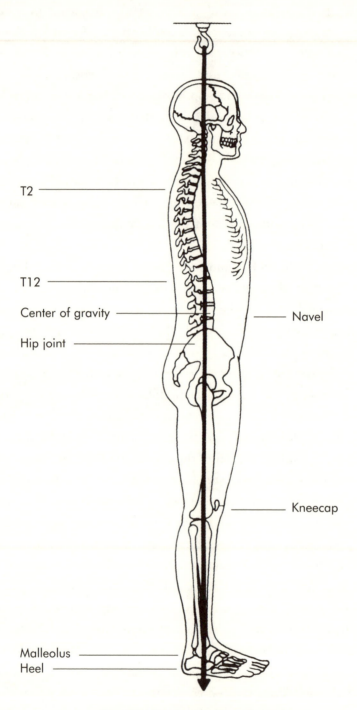

T2

T12

Center of gravity

Hip joint

Navel

Kneecap

Malleolus
Heel

Fig. 7.1. The body's line of gravity

of the navel. Its location varies according to body type, age, sex, attitude, breathing patterns, stress level, and neuromusculoskeletal alignment.

The most economical use of energy in the standing position occurs when the vertical line of gravity falls through a column of supporting bone. If weight-bearing bony segments are aligned so that the gravity line passes directly through the center of each joint, the least stress is placed upon the adjacent ligaments, tendons, and muscles. When this alignment is achieved, the antigravity muscles, which expend much energy to resist the downward pull of gravity, need not work as hard. The bones now take on a more active role in supporting our bodies in an upright posture, allowing the muscles to relax and rest, thus conserving energy and diminishing stress and tensions developed from unbalanced bone and muscle patterns.

Health potentials can be realized only when balance of structure exists so that both nerve energy and chi flow freely.

There are many negative health effects produced when these antigravity muscles are working either too much or too little. Muscles function to move bones. If muscles are either very tense or too flaccid, unilaterally or bilaterally, they will create a derangement in our bone structure. When people feel knots or spasms in their muscles it means that the given muscle has gone into a state of sustained contraction, meaning the muscle fibers are continuously shortened. As this occurs, bones can be pulled out of their proper alignment. When spinal vertebrae are involved in this structural imbalance nerve roots can be irritated, thus interfering with the function of the nervous system. When the nervous system experiences such interference a multitude of health problems can arise, since the nervous system is the means by which all body functions are regulated and monitored.

Health potentials are enhanced when proper communication between the brain and all body parts is maximized. Since this is the function of the nervous system, the structural integrity of our musculoskeletal system is of prime importance. Structure determines function.

Of course, other factors such as emotions, toxins, and trauma affect a person's structure as well. Muscles harbor tension and stress from various sources, but it is structural imbalance that is the end result. In turn, our functionability is diminished, as is our health.

From this standpoint a person must seriously consider how to go about producing optimum structural integrity in a balanced way. To do this, it is necessary to understand the value in learning about alignment; learn the principles from a competent source; recognize one's own problems in this area; and then apply the knowledge to oneself.

As a chiropractor I am concerned with correcting each patient's structure to allow the body's optimum function to be restored. But I can only do so much for a person. In reality, a person's health is his or her own responsibility. This is the reason it is vitally important for each person to learn about structure and to recognize what is right or wrong in his or her body. Such knowledge is essential for good health. I believe that some of the major keys to good health are proper bone alignment, muscle balance (symmetry), flexibility of joints and fascia, proper breathing, relaxation, and proper body utilization. Finally, of extreme importance is learning how to build and store chi, life-force energy that is usually wasted when structural imbalance exists.

Exercise is an indispensable means to attaining these keys to health. The exercise must not be one-sided, or unilateral, as most sports are, and must not produce tension. Well-toned muscles and fascia are desirable, but it is important to strike a balance: not too much tone or not too little. Balance is really the key when choosing an exercise system. The exercise system should be one that develops the body symmetrically, reduces stress, teaches proper alignment, and teaches how to store, increase, and conserve vital energy.

I am a chiropractor who sees health to a great extent dependent on symmetry or balance of body structure and so I became interested in the Chinese art of Iron Shirt Chi Kung. Iron Shirt emphasizes the importance of maintaining posture in such a way that the gravitational forces acting to push us down to Earth can be transmitted through the bones into the Earth rather than wasting energy resisting with the muscles or putting undue stress on the joints. The Iron Shirt postures align the vertebrae in such a manner as to permit the line of gravity to pass through the center of the vertebrae. Now the force is not being resisted but rather transmitted. The muscles, ligaments, and tendons can relax instead of working to resist.

The Iron Shirt postures integrate all structural tissues to produce optimum functioning. Relaxation, proper breathing, symmetrical muscle development, tendon and ligament strengthening, and strengthening of the bones result from Iron Shirt practice.

Another important concept is to learn to experience and re-create one's proper center of gravity. I say "proper" because generally a person's center of gravity changes from the navel area up into the chest or higher as one confronts life situations and stresses. This interferes with normal breathing patterns, which should be originating from the abdomen as well as the chest.

You simply have to compare a child's breathing to the breathing of most adults and it will become evident that adults mainly breathe from their chests, with very little abdominal or diaphragmatic action. It is important that we utilize our diaphragm when breathing, since the diaphragm descends upon and massages our internal visceral organs. This action enhances circulation and blood flow as well as increases oxygen transport to all of our vital organs.

The increased energy, structural integrity, and phenomenal health benefits gained from Iron Shirt practice are, in my opinion, outstanding. I feel that Iron Shirt practice can develop future health potential in a holistic way: physically, mentally, emotionally, and spiritually. Aligning yourself with Iron Shirt practice, you align yourself with the universe in all of its harmonious functioning.

FASCIA: PROTECTOR OF OUR VITAL ORGANS

After an ovum is fertilized it differentiates into three main systems: the ectoderm, the endoderm, and the mesoderm. The body's fascia is derived from the mesenchyme, which is a subdivision of the mesoderm.

Nuclei in the mesenchymal substance give rise to bones, ligaments, muscles, and tendons. Then a more structureless system of casings, sheaths, and tissue takes shape around the various centers that have been developed.

The fascia is a sheath and its function is that of support, protection, mechanical advantage, some degree of contractility and lengthening, and energizing the organs and muscles to let chi energy flow through easily. Fascia is a type of connective tissue that is avascular (without blood vessels); it is translucent and tough. It is intimately involved with muscles, encasing them and enhancing their duties by various means, including separating the muscle fibers into distinct bundles, providing bonds of especially tough fibers to offer support for purposes of leverage, and allowing for lubrication by means of fluids released from the tissues of an organ or part so that these enclosed muscle groups can slide over each other. Fascia is present throughout the body, separating, connecting, wrapping, and supporting various parts of the body and finally, on a superficial level, encasing the whole body in a shimmering sheath just beneath the level of the skin.

The superficial fascia is very resilient, due to the fact that the fibers run in a crisscross pattern. Damage by trauma alters the fibers, making them denser and shorter, a characteristic of scar tissue.

Since the fascial network is present throughout the body, it might explain the mechanism of trigger points, whereby the malfunction of internal organs is evidenced as pain in small areas often quite remote from the organ involved. This might also explain another mechanism, the one found in reflexology. Certain areas of the feet might at varying times be painful, coinciding with organs in the body.

There is another little-recognized function of fascia: that of providing muscle tone. In fact, low blood pressure is associated with a hypotonus condition of fascia and hypertension with a hypertoned fascia. This means that a condition of the fascia exists in which a high or low pressure causes too much or a limited diffusion of solutions throughout the fascia.

There are several types of fascia, all built of collagen. The most widely distributed is the loose connective tissue, which is the most flexible and most elastic of all, its fibers going in all directions. Loose connective tissue consists of protein embedded in a liquid ground substance; it is very important to water metabolism and other fluid exchanges in the body.

Tough, fibrous tissue can be found in areas where more tensile strength is required. Here the tissue is relatively unyielding, resulting from the parallel arrangement of bundles of fibers that are also found in tendons and ligaments. Huge fascial sheets found in the body are comprised of such tissue. All variations in fascia, however, stem from the mesoderm.

The fascia, though avascular itself, furnishes support for blood vessels, nerve fibers, and vessels of the lymphatic system and contains the nerves that convey fluid into the veins and sensory receptors, which are responsive to internal stimuli from the muscles, joints, and tendons. The fascia is also responsible for maintaining the relative positions of the various organs and muscles in the body.

Fascia exists in three layers. The superficial or subcutaneous layer is the layer beneath the skin. It is composed of two subdivisions: a layer that can contain a tremendous amount of fat in those who are overweight; and the more internal area of the subcutaneous fascia. This layer is the most elastic of the various fasciae, since it has to accommodate varying amounts of fat storage, swelling when there is inflammation and during muscular activity. This is the layer in which we are able to store chi energy. As this layer of the body fills up with chi, that area is unavailable for fat storage. By practicing Iron Shirt packing you can burn the fat that already exists out of this fascial layer.

The deep fascia, which is denser tissue with a smooth surface, reduces friction as one surface slides over another. The deep fascia produces bundles of fibers in parallel arrangement, giving great tensile strength. This sort of tissue is formed around the ankles, knees, wrists, and elbows, where it acts as an anchor against which muscles can pull. Fascia also acts in the capacity of a nutritional storehouse, as a source of insulation and support by means of fatty content, and as a barrier to impede the entrance of foreign organisms and objects.

The deep fascia keeps muscles in their distinct shapes and positions. This fascia, which is the densest and has the greatest tensile strength, is made up of three types. The first and outermost is the external surrounding layer, which covers large muscle groups. The intermediate membranes separate individual muscles; finally, the internal surrounding layer covers the external surfaces of the body cavities.

Internal to the intermediate membrane lies the subserous fascia. This is the fascial layer beneath the membranes of the body that lines all of the large cavities of the body. There are two types of subserous fascia: the parietal (or cavity wall) fascia, which covers the inner surfaces of the body cavities, such as the thorax or abdomen; and the visceral (or internal organ) fascia, which covers the organs in those cavities, such as the lungs or liver. The main functions of these tissues are protection and support, as well as providing a means of lubrication. During irritation these serousal surfaces sometimes adhere to one another, causing great pain.

Iron Shirt is primarily concerned with the subcutaneous (beneath the skin) layer of fascia, which covers the whole body. Iron Shirt is specifically concerned with the fascia in the lumbar region, which is thicker and more fatty than in other parts of the body. These two divisions of fasciae are joined by spindle connections, columnar-shaped fibers between which the fat is deposited.

The lumbar fascia is composed of three layers. The most superficial layer extends out from the middle, from the spinous processes of the lumbar vertebrae and the spine of the sacrum, constituting the back part of the pelvis and the sacrospinalis ligament, a ligament which extends vertically along the length of the vertebrae in that area, and the sides of the pelvis, where it joins with the intermediate layer of fascia. The intermediate layer extends from the middle of the area of the lumbar spine and out to the sides, where it joins with the superficial layer. These layers envelop the muscles that hold a person erect.

The fascial layers also extend upward to the lower portion of the twelfth rib and are attached to the iliac crest (the large upper part of the pelvis) and the iliolumbar ligament, both in the area of the small intestine. The deepest layer envelops the quadratus lumborum, a muscle that extends out from the area of the lumbar spine to join the fascial layers at the sides. The three layers together comprise what is technically known as the origin of the transverse abdominis aponeurosis.

The deep fascia of the upper back is made up primarily of thoracic fascia, which is a thin covering of the extensor muscles of the thoracic spine. Its lower border joins with the most superficial part of the tri-layer of the deep lumbar fascia while its upper portion combines with the cervical and trapezius fasciae. Attaching along a midline composed of the spines of the thoracic vertebrae, the deep fascia of the upper back extends out to the sides following the rib angles and the fascia of the muscles between the ribs.

The deep fascia that encloses the rhomboids (the muscles that attach to each shoulder blade) and muscles of the back is considered to be separate from the thoracic fascia, though there is no actual separation between the two.

Out to either side is the axillary fascia (covering the armpit), serving as a protective layer over the axillae, which are practically devoid of muscular tissue. The axillary fascia also partially encloses the back and side muscles, blends in with the thoracic fascia, and is connected to the fascia beneath the spine. In turn the deltoid fascia (covering the triangular muscle of the shoulder and upper arm), at about the level of the fourth thoracic vertebra and the mid-scapular (mid-shoulder blade) line, connects with the fascia beneath the spine and is anchored to the spine and the acromion process (the projection of the shoulder blade that forms the points of each shoulder).

All of the various layers just mentioned combine to form the continous fascial network of the back.

The deltoid fascia extends out from the spine at the scapulae to the clavicle (the collar bone). There it merges with the pectoral fascia (covering the breast). The deltoid fascia also extends laterally from the shoulder into the arm, where it becomes known as the brachial fascia. The brachial fascia joins with the pectoral and axillary fasciae and is attached to the epicondyles of each humerus (the large rounded prominences associated with the shoulder joints) on the upper end of the bone of the upper arm as well as the olecranon of each ulna (the curved part of the ulna bone at the point of the elbow). (The ulna bone is one of two bones in the forearm and is on the same side as the pinky finger. The other forearm bone is called the radius.) The brachial fascia is thin where it covers the biceps and thicker over the triceps.

The interbrachial fascia joins as one with the brachial fascia and extends from the epicondyles of the humerus to the remotest ends of the radius and ulna bones.

The pectoral fasciae are thin sheaths connected to the clavicle and sternum (the breastbone) and extends to the deltoid, brachial, and axillary fasciae and also the outer surrounding layer of the abdominal fascia. They also attach to the diaphragm. Beneath the pectoral fasciae lie the pectoralis major muscles. Beneath those are fascial sheaths called the clavipectoral fasciae that enclose the pectoralis minor muscles. This is found between the pectoralis minor and the thoracic body wall.

These fasciae, attached to the clavicle and enveloping the artery running beneath the clavicle, extend to the first rib, the coracoid process of the scapula (the bone that unites with the scapula to form the cavity through which the arteries of the scapula and temporal bones run), and the axillary fascia.

The ribs comprise the foundation of the thoracic body wall and are covered exteriorly by the external intercostal fascia (or fascia between the ribs). This sheath, extending in the direction of the head, joins the scalene fascia (the fascia covering the deep muscles attached to the cervical vertebrae and first and second ribs, acting to flex or bend the neck). Extending downward toward the lower abdomen, this sheath joins with the fascia that separates the external and internal oblique muscles of the abdomen.

The interior surfaces of the ribs are covered by the endothoracic fascia (surrounding the muscles within the thorax). This extends toward the head, blending with the prevertebral fascia (covering the vetebrae that are at the top of the spinal column), while in its extension to the lower abdomen it connects to the internal surrounding layer of the abdominal wall. The subcutaneous fascia of the abdomen is soft and pliable, increasing in tensile strength as it extends out to the sides. The highly elastic deeper portion of the subcutaneous fascia is attached to the linea alba and the inguinal (or groin) ligament. The outer layers of the deep abdominal fascia unite with the fasciae of the back and the breast. In their extension downward they connect with the fascia lata (the external fascia of the thighs), symphysis pubis (the junction of the two bones that join with a third to form the arch on either side of the pelvis), and the aponeurosis (the white fibrous tissue that forms the attachment of the external abdominal oblique muscles).

The surrounding internal layer unites with the deepest portion of the thoracolumbar fascia, the pelvic fascia, and the fascia of the diaphragm and together they are commonly referred to as the transversalis fasciae. These cover the external surface of the abdominal cavity wall, the lumbar vertebra bodies, and the psoas major muscle.

The various fascial layers that have been described are integral to the cultivation of Iron Shirt as the fascia into which we pack chi. As described, this chi will then form a protective cushion in the body that is also a storage place from which chi can be retrieved when required.

CLEANSING THE MARROW/
CHANGING THE TENDONS

The process of transforming sexual energy for storage in the brain and bone marrow, cleansing the internal organs, and restoring the organs to proper function is known as Cleansing the Bone Marrow.

By circulating chi in the Microcosmic Orbit and cleansing the inner marrow (which, as described in chapter 1, increases the quantity of blood cells, a vital source of life-force energy), your system is cleansed of pollution. With the routes cleared, chi flows freely to where it is needed and then it is said that the whole body is filled with chi.

When a person ages the bone marrow begins to dry out and produces fewer blood cells. At that time the body fills the empty space within the bones with fat. In order to fill the empty bones with renewed energy to revitalize the marrow to a youthful condition, we need to transfer sexual energy, which can be stored in the bones, while simultaneously burning out fat.

Cleansing the bone marrow, maintaining healthy organs, and changing the tendons lead to a strengthening of the muscles, tendons and ligaments, a condition described as one in which the inside of the body is clean and the outside is strong. All three levels of Iron Shirt practice are involved with strengthening and rebuilding the fascia, tendons, and bone marrow.

Using various methods, chi can be gathered from internal organs and led out to the fasciae surrounding them whenever necessary. When sufficient chi has been accumulated, it is guided out along the fascia between muscle groups and finally to the tendons that themselves are included in fascial sheaths until the entire body is filled with energy.

Tendons, the fibrous tissue that connects muscles to bones, are stronger than muscles and last longer. Fewer cells and smaller blood supplies are required to maintain and develop the tendons. Iron Shirt is designed to strengthen and develop the tendons so that movement no longer depends strongly upon the muscles.

In Taoism your health is said to be impaired if your tendons are crooked, loose, or weak. Diseased and crooked tendons will cause you to be thin; if the tendons are no longer resilient, this causes you to be easily fatigued as well. The fascia can become restricted due to injury, resulting in scar tissue, which is tough and tends to contract and pull upon the surrounding tissues and tendons, impeding blood flow and interfering with the passage of chi. Emotions can also be traumatic and can chronically alter your way of seeing the world and, thereby, the way in which you present yourself to the world. This is evident in many ways, most obviously by the way in which you hold yourself physically.

Fascia and tendons take a longer time to grow and, when injured, take a much longer time to heal. When, however, the tendons are strong, relaxed, and long and full of strength, they are also full of large quantities of chi and have ready access to more of it when needed. Once developed, they will be much stronger, last longer, and work harder. They will use very little nutrients and will require very little maintenance.

Some therapists have worked on loosening what has become overly restricting fascial tissue, thus often liberating emotions and memories that had created a constant drain on a person's energy reserves. Sometimes the person experiences a new lease on life by being able to function with a range of freedom of motion that he might otherwise never have known.

Changing the Tendons and Cleansing the Bone Marrow are the focus of teachings in Iron Shirt II and Iron Shirt III, respectively.

HARMONY OF FASCIA, TENDONS, AND CHI

A Taoist would describe the body as internally consisting of the vital internal organs and the chi energy that services them. Externally the body is comprised of bones, tendons, muscles, and the fasciae that contain them. Bones are moved by the action of muscle contractions, which create pulling forces on the tendons that are attached to the bones. Blood is said to move muscles and chi to move blood. Thus the Taoist master strives to create and protect the chi and the blood. This chi, as an electromagnetic energy, is unseen, while the muscles, tendons, bones, and fascia are quite visible. Practice consists of working both the visible and the invisible as an expression of the harmony of yin and yang.

To stress only internal or external development will result in disharmony and dysfunction. The organs and muscles must be vitalized by chi, but the circulation of that chi is augmented by having a healthy body. Strengthening muscles without cultivating chi creates a similar imbalance, which will not lead to true health or strength.

The practice of Changing the Tendons works with the muscles, tendons, bones, and fascia, developing both the visible (muscles, tendons, bones, and fascia) and the invisible (the flow of chi).

The practice of loosening the tendons is comparatively easy, whereas that of utilizing the fascia is considered to be more difficult. Iron Shirt Chi Kung is said to be the most difficult discipline of all martial arts and yet its practice, in which you learn to increase and store more chi, truly begins with the Microcosmic Orbit. Once you have collected chi you can direct it as it is needed to the fasciae of any point in the body.

By a process in which you collect, conserve, and reserve the energy of the vital organs (kidneys, brain, heart, liver, lungs, spleen and genitals), the polluted energy descends and exits as the clean, vital energy rises up to replace it. As you relax and collect more and more chi, it is directed toward the tendons and fascia until the entire body is filled with chi energy.

The chi flows into the fascia, expanding and strengthening the tendons.

Again, balance is necessary. If you practice so that your fascia is vitalized with chi but your tendons are neglected, the fascia will have nothing to depend on, since it is by way of the tendons that the muscles attach to the bones. On the other hand, if you work on the tendons and not the fascia, the fascia will not fill out and serve well as a coordinator of the muscle groups that it covers. If you exercise the tendons and the fascia without Chi Kung to activate an energy flow, the tendons and fascia will not "raise up" separately and will not be able to work freely. If you practice Chi Kung and not the tendon or fascia exercises, the chi will not be able to travel freely throughout the body and will be impeded in gaining access to all of the meridians. At the same time, the tendons will be weak through disuse and the fascia will be tight and restricting.

In this chapter, an overall picture is presented describing how the muscles, fascia, and bones function together. Muscles cover other muscles and bones and contain the various cavities that hold your vital organs. The tendons and fascia are joined together and the tendons connect muscles to bones. The fascia covers muscle groups, affording them the ability to do more work than they would were they not so bound together and add to the resilience and general tone of the muscles as well. Since these bundles of muscles wrapped in fascia lie outside of bones, they protect them; and since they make up the walls of the thoracic and abdominal cavities, they protect everything within them.

The most important purposes of Iron Shirt Chi Kung are to fill the cavities of the body with chi and to build up more chi pressure in the vital organs, protecting and enabling the organs to deliver instant energy.

MUSCLE-TENDON MERIDIANS

There are twelve muscle-tendon meridians in the body. These exist along the surfaces of the muscles and tendons, running from joint to joint. Unlike the meridians utilized in acupuncture and acupressure, the meridians do not connect with any internal organs. Muscle-tendon meridians originate in the extremities, meet at major joints, and end at points ranging throughout the torso and head. Knowing the routes of the muscle-tendon meridians and energizing them will greatly increase the muscle-tendon-fascia tone and improve range of motion.

Lung Muscle-Tendon Meridian

The lung muscle-tendon meridian (fig. 7.2) has its origin at the tip of the thumb. Looking at a person facing you with his arms at the sides of his body and the palms facing forward, the meridian would be seen as a line that extends up along the outer side of the bones of the thumb to the outside of the wrist. It then ascends up the outside of the forearm to the crook of the elbow. Rising up the biceps, it crosses over to and enters the chest, specifically to the sternoclavicular joint. From there it extends across the collarbone to the front deltoid, while another branch extends downward into the chest, sending still other branches down to the diaphragm.

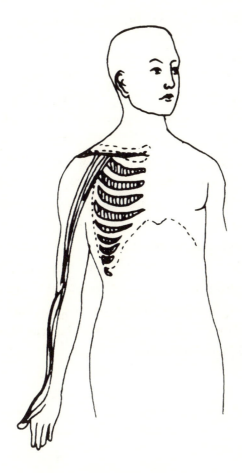

Fig. 7.2. Lung muscle-tendon meridian

Large Intestine Muscle-Tendon Meridian

Again, picture a person who is standing and facing you; this time his arms are at his sides, with the palms facing inward to the torso. The large intestine muscle-tendon meridian (fig. 7.3) begins at the end of the index finger and travels up along the outside of the forearm to the outer crook of the elbow. There it continues to ascend along the outside of the upper arm to the deltoid, where the meridian splits into two branches. One goes back over the trapezius muscle, descending down between the spinal column and scapula and then extending up along the spine to midway up the neck. The other branch travels across the lower surface of the trapezius and then to the sternocleido-mastoid muscle on its way to the face, where it splits again at the jaw line. One short branch runs to the corner of the nose; the other branch travels up along the side of the face, passing through the side of the forehead on its way over the top of the head and down a similar route to the opposite jaw, where it anchors.

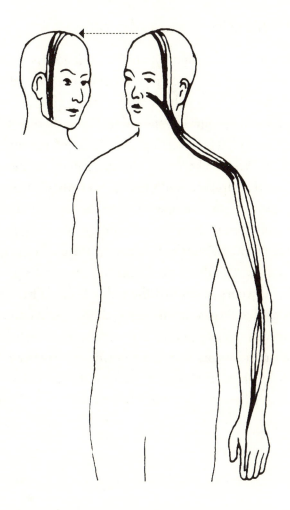

Fig. 7.3. Large intestine muscle-tendon meridian

Stomach Muscle-Tendon Meridian

The stomach muscle-tendon meridian (fig. 7.4) is somewhat more elaborate. It begins at the third toe (and sometimes the second toe and fourth toes as well). The meridian runs up the lower surface of the foot to about the level of the ankle. From there it splits into two branches. One branch travels up the middle of the lower leg to the outside of the knee. The other, running lateral to the first branch, continues to the hip joint and then up over the iliac crest (the upper part of the pelvis), continuing around to the back where it crosses the lower ribs and joins with an extension of the meridian that runs along the spine from the sacrum to the level of the collar bone.

The more medially located branch continues up to the top of the thigh and veers in toward the pubic bone. There it enters the abdomen and emerges again above the cavity of the collarbone. Next, it travels up the side of the neck and jaw, where it splits in two. One branch veers forward towards the corner of the mouth ascending up along the side of the nose to the corner of the eye. The other goes up along the jaw line to a point in front of the ear at the temple.

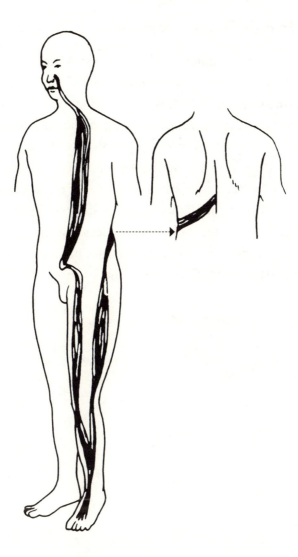

Fig. 7.4. Stomach muscle-tendon meridian

Spleen Muscle-Tendon Meridian

The spleen muscle-tendon meridian (fig. 7.5) originates at the middle and end of the big toe. It runs along the middle of the foot and ascends to the internal malleolus, the bone on each side of the ankle. From there it continues upward along the middle of the shin, passing through the middle of the knee and thigh and to end at a point on the groin. It then turns in toward the pubic bone and rises straight up to the navel. Veering off laterally, it crosses the abdomen, ending at a point just below the nipple, where it then enters into the chest. Another branch runs through a point located at the pubic bone to the coccygeal region, where it ascends the midline of the spine to approximately the level of the tops of the scapulae.

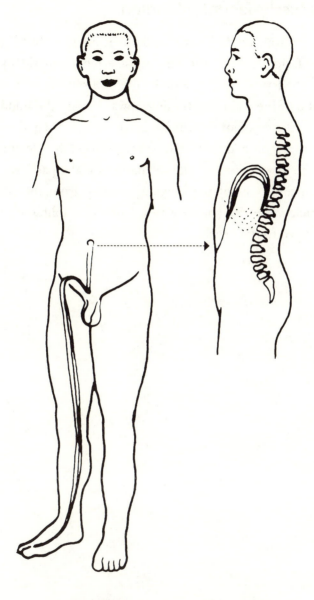

Fig. 7.5. Spleen muscle-tendon meridian

Heart Muscle-Tendon Meridian

With the person standing with his arms at the sides of his body and the palms facing forward, the heart muscle-tendon meridian (fig. 7.6) begins at the lateral tip of the pinky finger. From there it ascends to the middle of the wrist, continuing upward along the middle of the forearm to the crook of the elbow. Traveling upward and medially, it runs to the armpit and then crosses the pectoral muscle at about the level of the nipple, joins at the mediastinum (the partition between the two pleural sacs of the lungs, extending from the sternum to the thoracic vertebrae and downward to the diaphragm), and runs straight down to the navel.

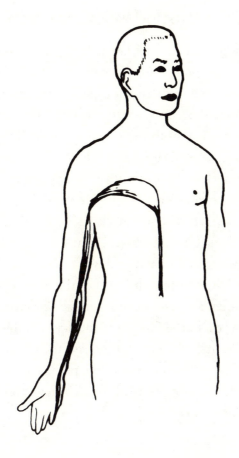

Fig. 7.6. Heart muscle-tendon meridian

Small Intestine Muscle-Tendon Meridian

With the person standing and facing away from you with his arms at the sides of his body and the palms facing forward, the small intestine muscle-tendon meridian (fig. 7.7) begins at the tip of the little finger. Ascending up along the back of that finger to a point on the wrist immediately above, it continues up along the middle of the forearm and proceeds up the middle of the upper arm. There it unites with its neck and ear extension behind the armpit. Ascending and descending, tracing out a sideways Z pattern, it continues up and over the trapezius, crossing the neck and connecting at the mastoid process, with a small branch entering the ear. Another branch loops up and over the ear and then dips down to end at a point on the jaw below that is slightly behind the level of the outer corner of the eye. The meridian then ascends, passing very close to the outer corner of the eye as it travels to the forehead, uniting with the muscle-tendon meridian extension of the mastoid process at the temple.

Still another branch issues out of the point at the mastoid process, ascending the previously described branch that crosses the forehead on its way to the temple.

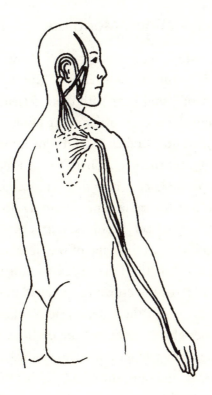

Fig. 7.7. Small intestine muscle-tendon meridian

Bladder Muscle-Tendon Meridian

Looking at a standing figure facing away from you, the bladder meridian (fig. 7.8) begins in the small toe. Running along the outer side of the foot, it rises and joins with the external malleolus. It then ascends to and joins the lateral corner of the popliteal fossa (the cavity behind the knee), while a branch extends downward from the external malleolus to join at the heel. Then it runs up along the calf and joins at the back of the knee. From there it ascends to the middle of the buttocks, while at the same time extending downward along the middle of the calf to the heel. From the buttocks it ascends along the midline of the backbone to the nape of the neck, continuing upward to join with the occiput (the lower back part of the skull). It then continues upward across the crown of the head to unite with a point at the side of the nose near the inner corner of the eye.

A branch arches along the line of the eyebrow and swoops down to the cheekbone. Then, continuing downward, it extends to the lower jaw, the throat, and onto the chest, passing under the armpit to angle up to and join with the line that ascends the backbone. A small branch extends up out of this extension to the backbone, rising at an angle out of the region of the scapula to unite in the shoulder. There is also a branch that extends out of the nape of the neck to unite with the root of the tongue. Finally, a short branch extends from the line coming up and out from under the armpit to join at the mastoid process.

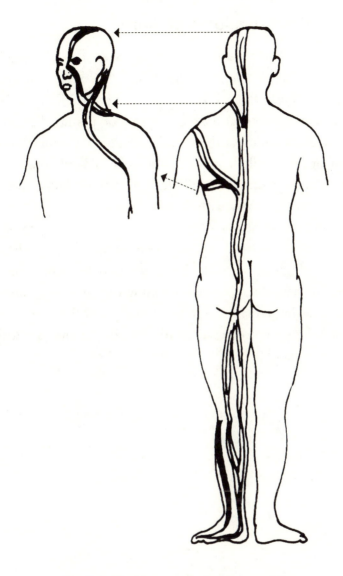

Fig. 7.8. Bladder muscle-tendon meridian

Kidney Muscle-Tendon Meridian

Looking at the back of a standing figure with the right heel lifted, the kidney muscle-tendon meridian (fig. 7.9) is seen to start under his little toe. From there it travels along the spleen muscle-tendon meridian and curves up at the arch of the foot, passing the underside of the ankle and uniting with the calf extension of the muscle-tendon meridian at the Achilles tendon. Continuing to ascend the middle of the calf, it unites again at the middle of the popliteal fossa (the cavity behind the knee), joining with the bladder meridian.

Viewing the same standing figure from the front, the kidney muscle-tendon meridian is seen to continue up along the inner side of the thigh, along with the spleen muscle-tendon meridian. It unites at the pubic bone, then continues a short way up to the navel. From the pubic bone it goes through to the coccyx, where it ascends the spine to connect with the occiput and join with the bladder meridian.

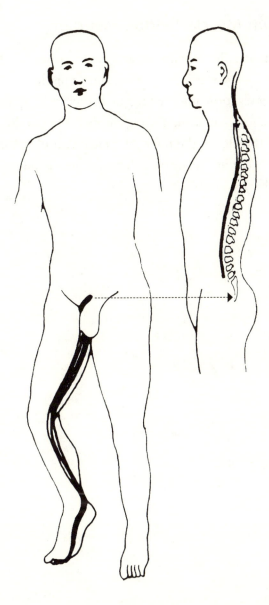

Fig. 7.9. Kidney muscle-tendon meridian

Pericardium Muscle-Tendon Meridian

Facing a standing figure with his arms at his sides and the palms of the hands facing forward, the pericardium muscle-tendon meridian (fig. 7.10) begins at the middle fingers. It then rises up the midline of the forearm and upper arm, passing through the middle of the palm, the crook of the elbow, the point of attachment of the front deltoid, and then into the armpit. From there it spreads out into the chest both ventrally and dorsally.

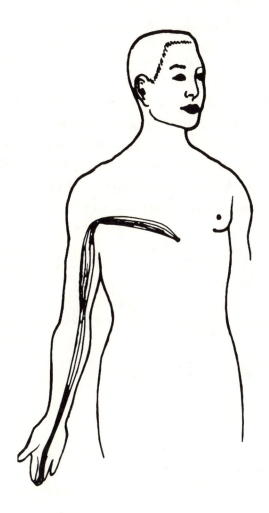

Fig. 7.10. Pericardium muscle-tendon meridian

Triple Warmer Muscle-Tendon Meridian

Observing a standing figure from the rear with his arms at his sides and the palms of the hands facing forward, the triple warmer muscle-tendon meridian (fig. 7.11) is seen to begin at the end of the fourth finger. It rises to a point directly above that finger at the wrist and travels up the forearm to the elbow. It travels up the middle of the upper arm and over the trapezius to the neck, where it joins the small intestine meridian. One branch goes to the jaw and connects with the root of the tongue, while the extension of the main meridian rises past the teeth to the ear. There it shifts forward to the outer corner of the eye and continues up past the temple to the upper part of the hairline.

Fig. 7.11. Triple warmer muscle-tendon meridian

Gall Bladder Muscle-Tendon Meridian

Here, when we view the figure from the side, we find that the gall bladder muscle-tendon meridian (fig. 7.12) begins at the outer side of the end of the fourth toe. From there it angles up along the lower leg, sending out a branch to the outer side of the knee. Continuing up the thigh, it disperses another branch at Stomach 32 and, continuing upward, sends out yet another branch that runs to the anus. It then ascends along the side of the body and rises in front of the shoulder, uniting with the muscle-tendon meridian extension that leads to the breast at the supraclavicular fossa. A slightly divergent point just below this bulges forward, where it links with the breast. The main meridian continues upward, rising up behind the ear to the crown of the head. It also descends in front of the ear to the side of the jaw; from there it ascends again to the corner of the nose, while another branch travels up to the outside corner of the eye.

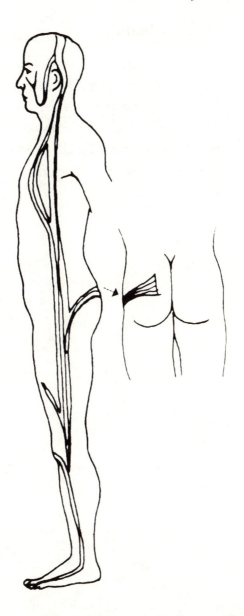

Fig. 7.12. Gall bladder muscle-tendon meridian

Liver Muscle-Tendon Meridian

Here we view the standing figure facing us. The liver muscle-tendon meridian (fig. 7.13) starts at the big toe and connects in front of the internal malleolus. It then rises up the lower leg along the tibia (the inner and larger of the two bones of the lower leg) and joins on the inner side of the knee. Finally, it sweeps up the thigh and unites at the pubic bone, thereby connecting with all of the other muscle meridians.

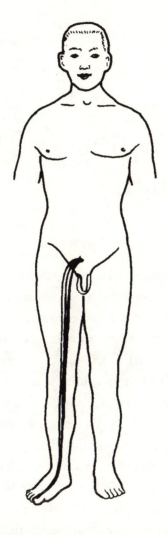

Fig. 7.13. Liver muscle-tendon meridian

Developing a Daily Practice

Practice the Iron Shirt exercises you have learned in this book. In a short time you will find that it all fits together quite easily and becomes as ordinary, and yet as necessary, as brushing your teeth. You will, in other words, begin another good habit. To develop the daily practice of Iron Shirt, it will serve you well to realize that you do not need to do all of the postures or breath-alignment exercises every day. On those days that you do practice, it is best to do so early in the morning when you arise. Design a schedule that works for you. You might be able to devote no more than five or ten minutes to an activity, but do it. Rising twenty minutes or a half hour earlier in the morning will improve your whole life. In fact, in a short time you will discover that you need less sleep and have more strength and energy. At the same time, you will find that your activities, both before and after practice, will become more efficient; you will therefore derive even more benefit from the practices, even though you spend what might seem like only a little time actually working with them.

You can create a schedule to fit your time allowance. A recommended schedule to follow might be:

Monday: Embracing the Tree for approximately six to seven minutes, followed by Holding the Golden Urn and the Horse Stance Using a Wall

Tuesday: Embracing the Tree, the Golden Turtle and the Water Buffalo, and the Horse Stance Using a Wall

Wednesday: Embracing the Tree, the Golden Turtle and the Water Buffalo, the Golden Phoenix, and Door Hanging

Thursday: Embracing the Tree, the Golden Phoenix, the Iron Bridge, and the Backbend

Friday: Embracing the Tree, the Iron Bridge, the Iron Bar, and the Warrior Poses

Saturday and Sunday: Embracing the Tree, or rest for both days before beginning the cycle again. You may also decide to start the schedule over on Saturday. It is important to remember to start gradually, practicing only fifteen or twenty minutes to a half hour per day.

Iron Shirt can be practiced at any time. Once you master using the mind to bring chi to the various parts of the organs, you will find it very useful and you will be able to use the chi energy anytime that you want or need it. If, for example, you are riding in a car, on a train, or in a plane and you feel back pain, you can bring the energy to the back by pulling up the anus and bringing the energy to the kidneys, or simply by contracting the back muscles. Squeeze and release, squeeze and release and you will find that the pain or stiffness will go away. You will feel energized immediately. In this way you can help the organs that need to be exercised.

Fit in some practice whenever you find some time during the day. It does not have to be any particular time and/or place. When you are standing on line, for example, with time on your hands, you can practice elongating the spine by pressing the legs down with the sensation of screwing them into the ground. Pull your head up at the same time and push the spine down. Once you master the practice, you can use it in any way that you want.

If you want to strengthen a particular muscle-tendon meridian, you can consult the timetable that shows when chi flow to the organs is strongest (fig. 8.1). For example, if you want to strengthen the large

Fig. 8.1. Timetable of chi flow to the organs

intestine muscle-tendon meridian, it is best to practice between 5:30 AM and 7:30 AM.

One warning about timing: Do not practice too close to bedtime or you will not be able to sleep.

If you practice the Six Healing Sounds (as described in *Taoist Ways to Transform Stress into Vitality*) just before going to bed, you will sleep more soundly and awaken earlier and more refreshed. Upon awakening, do not suddenly jump out of bed. Allow your engine (your body) to warm up a little first. Switching into high gear as soon as you get up can be disruptive and damaging to your entire system. Although you may experience vitality as soon as you awaken, if you are in the habit of bouncing out of bed when you wake up, lie in bed a while instead and practice the Inner Smile, allowing the energy to flow into your Microcosmic Orbit. You will be amazed at how much your health and overall progress will improve.

Continue with chi self-massage as described in *Chi Self-Massage: The Taoist Way of Rejuvenation*. If you are pressed for time, practice chi self-massage while taking your morning constitutional. It is not necessary to set aside time to do these practices, since you can combine them with other activities. After diligently spending time in the Universal Tao System, you will easily be able to realize differences in your general well-being.

You should drink some water when you wake up, but not to excess. Drink as much as is comfortable for you. Imbibing too much water can make you feel nauseated and can even damage your kidneys. For drinking purposes it is wise to use a water filter or to distill your water. Water and air are the two most important ingredients to good health and steady progress in the Universal Tao system. If you are worried about losing trace minerals through distillation, use tap water to cook with. Then you will receive your minerals, too. Make sure that the tap water is filtered, at least through a simple mesh. Whenever possible, make sure that the air that you breathe is filtered as well. Air filters equipped with ion emitters are best.

If you feel any discomfort during your practice, consult any Universal Tao certified instructor. If the problem still exists, consult a qualified physician. Remember that exercise is a tool. To misuse such a tool can be harmful. Iron Shirt Chi Kung is not meant to be harmful and it will not be if used in the proper way. The exercises have been clearly outlined, as well as the side effects and how to prevent them. If the instructions are followed properly there will be no problems.

Long life, good health, and good luck in developing your Iron Shirt!

About the Author

Mantak Chia has been studying the Taoist approach to life since childhood. His mastery of this ancient knowledge, enhanced by his study of other disciplines, has resulted in the development of the Universal Tao System, which is now being taught throughout the world.

Mantak Chia was born in Thailand to Chinese parents in 1944. When he was six years old, he learned from Buddhist monks how to sit and "still the mind." While in grammar school he learned traditional Thai boxing, and soon went on to acquire considerable skill in Aikido, Yoga, and Tai Chi. His studies of the Taoist way of life began in earnest when he was a student in Hong Kong, ultimately leading to his mastery of a wide variety of esoteric disciplines. To better understand the mechanisms behind healing energy, he also studied Western anatomy and medical sciences.

Master Chia has taught his system of healing and energizing practices to tens of thousands of students and trained more than two thousand instructors and practitioners throughout the world. He has established centers for Taoist study and training in many countries around the globe. In June 1990 he was honored by the International Congress of Chinese Medicine and Qi Gong (Chi Kung), which named him the Qi Gong Master of the Year.

The Universal Tao System and Training Center

THE UNIVERSAL TAO SYSTEM

The ultimate goal of Taoist practice is to transcend physical boundaries through the development of the soul and the spirit within the human. That is also the guiding principle behind the Universal Tao, a practical system of self-development that enables individuals to complete the harmonious evolution of their physical, mental, and spiritual bodies. Through a series of ancient Chinese meditative and internal energy exercises, the practitioner learns to increase physical energy, release tension, improve health, practice self-defense, and gain the ability to heal oneself and others. In the process of creating a solid foundation of health and well-being in the physical body, the practitioner also creates the basis for developing his or her spiritual potential by learning to tap into the natural energies of the Sun, Moon, Earth, stars, and other environmental forces.

The Universal Tao practices are derived from ancient techniques rooted in the processes of nature. They have been gathered and integrated into a coherent, accessible system for well-being that works directly with the life force, or chi, that flows through the meridian system of the body.

Master Chia has spent years developing and perfecting techniques for teaching these traditional practices to students around the world through ongoing classes, workshops, private instruction, and healing sessions, as well as books and video and audio products. Further information can be obtained at www.universal-tao.com.

THE UNIVERSAL TAO TRAINING CENTER

The Tao Garden Resort and Training Center in northern Thailand is the home of Master Chia and serves as the worldwide headquarters for Universal Tao activities. This integrated wellness, holistic health, and training center is situated on eighty acres surrounded by the beautiful Himalayan foothills near the historic walled city of Chiang Mai. The serene setting includes flower and herb gardens ideal for meditation, open-air pavilions for practicing Chi Kung, and a health and fitness spa.

The Center offers classes year-round, as well as summer and winter retreats. It can accommodate two hundred students, and group leasing can be arranged. For more information, you may fax the Center at (66)(53) 495-852, or email universaltao@universal-tao.com.

# Resources

For information worldwide on courses, books, products, and other resources, contact:

Universal Healing Tao Center
274 Moo 7, Laung Nua, Doi Saket, Chiang Mai, 50220, Thailand
Tel: (66)(53) 921-200
Email: universaltao@universal-tao.com
Website: www.universal-tao.com

For information on retreats and Health Spa, contact:
Tao Garden Health Spa & Resort
Email: reservations@tao-garden.com
Website: www.tao-garden.com

Good Chi • Good Heart • Good Intention

# Index